Called To Be Holy

Dear Kathryn,

This book has significantly challenged me this last year. In fact, it has been transformational in my walk with Jesus. It has pushed me to a deeper and purer place in Jesus in my heart. I really wanted to share it with you. The first couple of chapters are academic and contextually interesting. It gets more practical and personal as it progresses through Scripture. I pray it moves you closer to His truth, purpose and heart for you. I love you, Kathryn! Happy Birthday!

Colossians 1:28-29

Soli Deo Gloria,
Suzanne Edgar
January 2006

Called To Be Holy

John N. Oswalt

FRANCIS ASBURY PRESS
of Evangel Publishing House

Nappanee, Indiana 46550

Evangel Publishing House
2000 Evangel Way
P.O. Box 189
Nappanee, Indiana 46550

Toll-Free Order Line: (800) 253-9315
Website: www.evangelpublishing.com

Cover Design by Foster & Foster

Publisher's Cataloging-in-Publication
(Provided by Quality Books, Inc.)

Oswalt, John.
　　Called to be holy / John N. Oswalt – 1st ed.
　　p. cm.
　　Includes bibliographic references and index.
　　LCCN: 98-72661
　　ISBN: 0-916035-92-1

　　1. Holiness–Christianity. 2. Christian Life
I. Title
BT767.O89 1999

234'.8
QBI99-906

Printed in the United States of America

03 04 05 06 07 / 10 9 8 7 6 5 4 3

For Hule Goddard
and all my other students

Whose earnest questions made me think
through this material more clearly

Contents

PREFACE ix

INTRODUCTION: HOLINESS—THE NEED 1

PART ONE: THE OLD TESTAMENT

1. Holiness and Covenant 9
2. God's Holy Character as Seen in the Covenant 21
3. The Covenant and Human Nature 39
4. Life Expectations in the Old Testament 45
5. The Gift of the Holy Spirit in the Old Testament 65
6. The Spirit and the Messiah 89
7. The Old Testament and Holiness 97

PART TWO: THE NEW TESTAMENT

8. The New Covenant and the Holy Life 103
9. The Ministry of Jesus and the Life of Holiness 125
10. New Testament Expectations of Christian Life 135
11. How to Experience the Life of Holiness 149
12. Holiness and Sin 165

PART THREE: WALKING IN HOLINESS

13. Walking in Holiness 185

FURTHER READING 201
INDEX 203

Preface

The gestation period of this book has been an uncommonly long one. What I have written in these pages is the result of some 40 years of study, teaching, preaching and reflecting. In the end, this is what I believe about the subject of Christian holiness. In that sense, it is a deeply personal statement. These are not merely ideas, they are convictions. In their origins they go back to at least 1958 on the campus of Taylor University, Upland, Indiana where I came under the ministry of a man who was to have a profound influence over my life up till the present day. This man was Dr. Dennis F. Kinlaw. In the fall of 1958, Dr. Kinlaw came to Taylor University to preach for what was known as Spiritual Emphasis week. Under the influence of his preaching and through his wise personal counsel, I there surrendered my rebellious will to God, once and for all. That moment in a small counseling room in a long-gone dormitory has shaped, and will shape, all the rest of my life. It marked the end of one phase of my Christian experience, and the beginning of another. There began my quest for all that God could give me of his holiness. The quest is not over. There are yet more layers of my convoluted soul to be turned back and opened to God's cleansing light. But in the words of Dr. David Seamands, another man who has contributed so much to my thinking on this subject, "I have been forever ruined for sin."

Two other persons deserve to be mentioned here, both from college days. Dr. Jim Young taught me the necessity of rigorous honesty and integrity if the life of holiness is to mean anything at all. He also showed me what it is to give yourself away for others in an innocent joy in all of God's creation. Richard Baarendse was my classmate, and although not much older than me in years, he was much more mature in faith than I. Dick's passionate love for the Lord and his infectious joy in the Lord's service were beacon lights in those days and have remained so across the years. In Dick and in his wife-to-be, Elsbeth Baris, I saw holiness lived out.

In my third year of theological studies at Asbury Theological Seminary, Dr. Kinlaw joined the faculty. I believe I took every course he offered in the next two years. I shamelessly camped on his doorstep at home and on the threshold of his office, pestering him with questions, doubts, and not a few half-baked ideas. He made time for me and I saw in him an integration of deep personal faith and an inquiring mind that has been a model for me across the ensuing years. Since 1970 it has been my privilege to live in the same small town in Kentucky with Dr. Kinlaw, and this has afforded me many happy hours of challenging interaction with him on this subject and others. I owe him a debt that can never be repaid, except perhaps by mentoring other insistent youth such as I was.

I must mention one other person who has exercised great influence upon my life and thought. This is Dr. Allan Coppedge. Al came to the faculty of Asbury a few years after I did, and with the exception of three years when I and my family were living outside of Kentucky, he and I have prayed together on an almost-weekly basis ever since. In him I see a passion to know God and his ways and a passion to share that knowledge with others in self-denying ways. His example has increasingly come to represent to me what holiness looks like when it is incarnated.

In 1973 after I had returned to Asbury as a member of the faculty, I was asked to be one of the speakers in a conference on Christian Holiness. Here was the place where I could no longer be an inquirer but must begin to become a proclaimer. Some of the concepts in this book date to those lecture/sermons. Since those days I have preached and lectured on the subject in many places: The Japan Holiness Association, the Christian Holiness Association, and the Salvation Army, among others, and in those settings my thoughts were developed still further.

But the direct stimulus for putting all of these amassed ideas together was an invitation to deliver the annual Chamberlain Holiness Lectures at Wesley Biblical Seminary in Jackson, Mississippi in October 1994. While the lectures have been heavily revised and supplemented for the book format, I believe those who attended will recognize most of the content as it appears here. It is a pleasure to offer the book to the administration, faculty and students of Wesley Biblical Seminary in gratitude both for the invitation and for their many kindnesses to me during the week of lectures.

It remains to me to acknowledge the great debt I owe to Asbury Theological Seminary, which has been alma mater, spiritual stimulus and catalyst, platform, and not least, place of employment for 22 of the last 29 years. It is through the generosity of the Board of Trustees who have granted a sabbatical leave that this book was written. During that leave it was a great privilege to be in residence at Tyndale House, Cambridge, England. The staff and other residents extended themselves in kindness to make my wife's and my stay there an enjoyable and profitable one.

John N. Oswalt
Asbury Theological Seminary

INTRODUCTION

Holiness—the Need

The fate of the Christian Church in America and around the world depends upon what the Church does with the biblical doctrine of holiness. Such a radical statement immediately calls for some explanation. Why do I say such a thing, and exactly what do I mean by "the biblical doctrine of holiness"? Let me begin with the latter. What is the biblical doctrine of holiness? Since that is the fundamental focus of this book, I am not going to go into detail here, but I do want to give you, the reader, enough information to understand my opening statement.

The apostle Peter, writing in his first letter, says these words,

> Therefore, prepare your minds for action; be self-controlled; set your hope fully on the grace to be given you when Jesus Christ is revealed. As obedient children, do not conform to the evil desires you had when you lived in ignorance. But just as he who called you is holy, so be holy in all you do; For it is written, 'Be holy, because I am holy.' (1:13-16, NIV)

In these few words, Peter says a great deal. In the first place, he asserts the fundamental continuity between the Christian faith and the faith of Israel proclaimed in the Old Testament. He does so by quoting from the Old Testament in his final proof. Why should we be holy? Because of what God has said about himself and those who believe in him in the Old Testament. Peter believes that what is said in the Old Testament has immediate relevance for believers in Jesus Christ. But Peter also does something else, something that all the other New Testament writers do, but something that Peter summarizes well. In a few words, Peter shows the intimate connection between forgiveness and a life of holiness. He says that those who have received the grace of forgiveness through the death of Jesus Christ are expected to live lives that conform to the character of God, a character he defines using the biblical term "holy." And whatever else "holy" means, it is evidently in marked contrast to that life lived before receiving the grace of God, a life marked by conformity to "evil desires" lived in because of "ignorance." So what Peter is doing here is to carefully link the receiving of God's grace with a radically transformed life. Grace and transformation cannot be separated. To claim to have received God's forgiving grace while continuing to live a life that is dominated by the desires is a contradiction in terms. But someone will surely say, "This is to belabor the obvious. Everyone who knows anything about Christianity will certainly know that Christians are expected to live different lives after their conversion than before." That may be so. But I wonder how seriously modern Western Christians really do take that linkage?

So according to Peter what is the biblical doctrine of holiness? For him it has four components: (1) Holiness first of all defines a way of behaving; (2) It is a way of behaving which is determined by the character of God; (3) It is a way of behaving which all Christians are expected to manifest; and (4) It is a way of behaving which is markedly different from that of unbelievers. Of course, one passage from one New Testament letter would not by itself demonstrate that these four points are the normative teaching on the subject. That could only be true if this short statement was indeed a valid summary of what the Bible teaches on the subject. In fact, that is precisely the case, as I will attempt to demonstrate in the rest of the book.

So I am saying by my opening statement that the fate of the Church of Jesus Christ hangs on how seriously it takes the biblical teaching that Christians are to live lives which radically manifest the unique character of God. But why should I say such a thing? Yes, perhaps the fate of the Church hangs on what it does with the deity of Christ, or upon what it does with the uniqueness of the Gospel, or even upon what it does with the doctrine of the Trinity, but the doctrine of Christian holiness? Surely not! Surely the question of the Bible's teaching on holiness is one of those secondary issues like church government or the relation of the rapture to the Second Coming of Christ, where we can agree to disagree, realizing that the survival of the faith hardly depends upon one particular resolution to these vexed questions.

But no, the importance of the Bible's teaching on holiness is not comparable to its teachings on ecclesiology or eschatology. And the reason is this: the Christian gospel is not primarily about having one's sins forgiven and spending a blissful eternity with God after somehow getting through this life with one's faith reasonably intact. This view, which I do not hesitate to call heretical, is the result of a misreading of the New Testament. If a person constantly reads the New Testament in the light of the Old, which the Church Fathers clearly intended by their joining of the two in one canon, then it becomes unmistakably clear what the purpose of the Gospel is. It is the same purpose that God has had from Genesis 4 onwards: the transformation of human behavior in this world with the consequent possibility of living with God through all eternity. The Old Testament shows us what that transformation is, and the New Testament shows us what God has done to make the transformation possible.

This means that unless Christians are truly transformed into the character of God, the whole purpose of the Church's existence becomes blurred and confused. The world looks upon hateful, self-serving, undisciplined, greedy, impure people who nevertheless claim to be the people of God, and says, "You lie!" But beyond this, a Church without the character of God lacks the power of God, and we find ourselves right back in the situation in which Israel found itself:

> We were with child, we writhed in pain, but we gave birth to wind. We have not brought salvation to the earth, we have not given birth to people of the world. (Isa. 26:18)

> We look for justice, but find none; for deliverance, but it is far away. For our offenses are many in your sight, and our sins testify against us. Our offenses are ever with us, and we acknowledge our iniquities: rebellion and treachery against the LORD, turning our backs on our God, fomenting oppression and revolt, uttering lies our hearts have conceived. So justice is driven back, and righteousness stands at a distance; truth has stumbled in the streets, honesty cannot enter. (Isa. 59:11b-14)

By contrast, when the holy character of God is seen in broken, fallible people it is apparent that something supernatural has taken place in them. And this becomes a sign of hope to the world that their sinful condition can be addressed as well. This is what Ezekiel is talking about when he says: "Then the nations will know that I am the LORD, declares the Sovereign LORD, when I show myself holy through you before their eyes" (Ezek. 36:23).

In the post-World War II era, American Christendom has increasingly stressed what Dietrich Bonhoeffer in his book *The Cost of Discipleship* called "cheap grace." It is the Reformation teaching *sola gratia* run amok. Luther rediscovered the truth which the Roman church had lost in the Dark Ages: there is nothing we humans can do to earn the grace of God. There is only one thing we can do to enter a restored relation between ourselves and the Father. That one thing is to believe God's declaration that Jesus Christ has died for our sins. We do not have to be good enough for God; we do not have to clean ourselves up for him. In fact, we can do neither of those. We are saved from our sin through God's grace alone—*nothing* else. What good news this is, both to those who have been raised in a Christian environment and those who have not.

All too often those raised in a Christian environment have had impressed upon them the need to be "good." And thus they have concluded, usually quite unconsciously, that God will only accept them if they are "good." And this becomes a heavy burden as they try to be good enough for God. What good news to hear that the benefits of Christ's cross are free! What good news it is that we can be forgiven and given a new life apart from our performance.

By the same token free grace is good news for those who have not been raised in a Christian environment, persons who may feel that they have been too "bad" ever to be able to deserve God's love. To such persons it is a wonderful relief to hear that God's forgiveness does not depend on anything we have done to deserve it.

So what is the problem? What do I mean when I say that "grace alone" has run amok in modern American Christendom. It is the very problem which the Apostle Paul anticipated and addressed in Romans chapters 6-8. If there was nothing I could do to receive God's grace, then there is nothing I need to do to remain in that grace. In fact, if I periodically fall from it, I will receive it all the more. To all of that Paul said, "God forbid!" Paul, like Peter, understood from his Old Testament roots that God's grace was meant not only to deliver us from the guilt of sin, but also from its power. We have lost sight of this truth. We have been taught that while Christians should fight against sin, they cannot help but engage in it. Thus we should not be at all surprised when our leaders fall into embezzlement, adultery, substance-abuse, and the like. We expect to live in sin and all our expectations are fulfilled with a vengeance.

Am I suggesting that we are saved from the guilt of sin by grace and from the power of sin by effort? Not at all! The problem with "cheap grace" is that it does not go far enough. It fails to understand that the goal of God's grace is nothing less than Christlikeness. We want to believe God to escape the consequences of our sin, but we do not want to believe Christ to deliver us from our sinning. We want to enjoy the pleasure of sin while escaping its bitter consequences. But the Scriptures call us to a life which is radically Christlike, or to say it another way, one which has been transformed into the character of God. This is the goal of the gospel, the goal of grace.

The Church which has lost sight of the biblical doctrine of holiness tries to market the gospel as a solution for life's difficulties, a source for personal fulfillment, a means of achieving one's desires for significance and status and power. In other words, it is not a means of escaping the rule of desire, it is a means for *fulfilling* that rule. It suggests to people that they need not forsake their favorite sins, that indeed they cannot, but that they can find continuing forgiveness from a God who knows nothing of justice but everything of a sentimental feeling misnamed "love." It is a Church that expects to go down the aisle to meet its Bridegroom in a dress as filthy as the one in which He first found her in the gutters of life. It is a Church that will not survive the fires of the coming Tribulation.

Will there be a Church that survives those fires! Oh yes! God guarantees it. But it will be one that has believed its Lord for grace to forgive *and* for grace to purify. It will love its Lord in spite of deprivation, loss, and lack of fulfillment. It will, in the words of Paul, gladly lose all things in order to gain Christ (Phil 3:8). Its goal will not be the fulfillment of the desires for pleasure, possessions and power, but that Christ may be formed in it (Gal. 4:19).

I conclude as I began: The fate of the American church and the Church around the world depends upon what it does with the biblical doctrine of Christian holiness.

PART ONE

THE OLD TESTAMENT

1

Holiness and Covenant

If we are to understand the biblical doctrine of holiness, we must begin with the Old Testament. It is there that we learn what the human problem really is, and how God intends to solve that problem. It is also there that we learn what the human character is and what God's character is. The New Testament writers assume that their readers have access to the Old Testament and that they understand its content. Therefore, the writers do not go into detail on the above issues. They do not say much about the fundamentally perverse nature of humanity. Neither do they speak much about the transcendence, justice, and holiness of God. They do say a good deal about God's ultimate purpose of transformed character, but unless you have already been sensitized by reading the Old Testament, it is easy to overlook this and focus solely upon forgiveness.

Thus, when we read the New Testament alone, we are reading an incomplete book. It is as though we have a manual on a complex machine. The manual is in two parts. The first part explains how the machine is constructed and how it accomplishes its work. The second part of the manual explains how to operate the machine. But the second part is written under the assumption that we have read the first part. If we have only read the second part, we may not understand why some steps are specified and may not even realize they are there. We may overlook them entirely, not because we mean to, but simply because we don't recognize the need for them.

That is what has happened to much of the modern Church. Having dismissed the Old Testament as "preliminary," or as "background," or even as "sub-Christian," we have come to teach God as a sentimental, but useful grandfather figure, who in the words of a popular song of another generation "will always say 'I forgive.'" He places no demands upon us and functions primarily to answer our prayers. By the same token our faith is primarily a matter of individual relations with God which involve few if any community obligations. In direct defiance of the words of Christ in Matthew 5:48, we announce from our bumpers and our lapels, "Christians aren't perfect, just forgiven."

If the Church is to be all that it is called to be, we must begin to read the two parts of the Bible in the light of each other. If we read the Old Testament apart from the New, we will almost certainly misread it and come to believe with Judaism that one comes into a saving relationship with God through works of obedience. We need to hear Jesus and Paul telling us, "No, that's not what it is about at all." And the same is true for the New Testament. If we read it apart from the exposition of the human problem and the divine character found in the Old Testament, there is a very good chance we will come to believe that the only significance of Christ's death was to procure forgiveness for us humans.

The Structure of the Covenant and the Revelation of God

So how does the Old Testament go about showing us the character of God, the nature of the human predicament, and God's intentions for his people? Above all, it does so through the mechanism of a covenant. A covenant in the Old Testament world was a solemn agreement between two parties. Each one accepted certain obligations to the other and in return received certain benefits from the other. The form which the Bible uses is very similar to one which the Hittite rulers of 1500-1200 B.C. used with their subject peoples. We might ask why God did this. Why use a secular political form to show his people who he is and what they are?

The answer to that question lies in the nature of God and of ancient world religion. The religions of the ancient Near East were remarkably similar in their basic concepts. This is true from southern Babylon in the east to Italy in the west, and from Egypt in the south to the Caucasus in the north. It extends from the time of Sumer as shown in the very earliest written records of 3000 B.C. to the final fall of Roman religion, to Christianity in 300 A.D. It continues to exist today, particularly in Hinduism, and in its western clone, the New Age movement.

Those common concepts were these:

1. Everything that exists, whether human, natural, or divine, is continuous with everything else that exists. Thus, all psycho-socio-physical phenomena are identified with the divine, and there are as many different gods and goddesses as there are phenomena.

2. Good is understood as that which is supportive of cosmic order and evil is that which is destructive of that order. Good and evil are cosmic principles which are in endless conflict.

3. The formation of the visible world is the result of this cosmic conflict between constructive and destructive principles.

4. Matter, in the form of watery chaos, has always existed.

5. The gods emerged from this material, primarily through sexual means.

6. The character of the gods is identical with that of humans, only on a grander scale. They are strong, but weak; faithful, but deceptive; loving, but hateful; dependable, but fickle.

7. The gods are bound by no code of honor. That is, they need not be supportive of their worshippers if they choose not to be. However, each god is bound by his or her fate. They cannot escape what is decreed for them. So, many of them endlessly die, often tragically, and are reborn.

8. This fate is not determined by the gods, but is independent of them. Thus, it may be said that if there is an absolute in this understanding of reality, that absolute is impersonal power.

9. Because of the identity among the human, natural, and divine realms, what is done in one realm must infallibly produce the same results in the other realms, unless some destructive force has disrupted the identity in some way. Thus, the means of affecting nature and the gods is always through sympathetic magic.

10. Since the gods are identical with humans, the fundamental life force is sexual. Sex is a profoundly religious activity, whereby the continued life of the cosmos is assured.

11. Since the human world is identical with the divine world, and since the divine world is necessarily the more significant of the two, the human world must then be only a reflection of the invisible reality.

12. If the human and natural worlds are reflections of invisible reality, then reality has no purpose except survival, and it has no goal except continued existence. In other words, reality is circular, coming from nowhere and going nowhere.

13. There is no such thing as absolute ethics. Obviously, that is an impossibility in a polytheistic environment where all the gods adhere to differing ethical standards. Furthermore, ethics have little bearing on one's relationship to the gods. Ethical standards are the province of the king, because they are a practical necessity for human society to exist. Typically, the king claims to have gotten the standards from a god, but adhering to them has no real connection with religious behavior.

14. Religion has as its purpose the maintenance of the great cycles of existence with a minimum of disruption. It does so by magically strengthening the hand of the constructive forces and weakening the hand of the destructive forces. One aspect of this process is to act out stories of the gods in which these results are achieved.

15. In such an understanding, humanity is of a very low value, and individual humans and their experiences are of no value at all. They are only of value to the degree that they conform to the ideal. Unique events and persons are valueless because they are not seen to contribute to the recurring cycles of nature and existence.

This is the understanding of reality that prevailed all around the people of Israel, and especially in Egypt, where the Israelites spent some 400 years, the latter part as slaves. But the Bible shows us that this understanding of reality is almost diametrically wrong. On virtually every point enumerated above, the Biblical understanding is radically different:

1. There are fixed boundaries between God and the cosmos he created. He is not the cosmos, and he is not to be identified with it. Since there can be only one such transcendent Creator, he is the only God.

2. Good is that which is consistent with God's creative will, and evil is that which is not consistent with his will. They are not eternal principles that exist apart from God.

3. The cosmos has not come into existence because of conflict between eternal principles. It came into existence because God willed it, and it did so in harmony and serenity.

4. God, who is a personal spirit, is the only entity that has always existed.

5. Matter came into existence because God spoke it into existence.

6. God's character is radically different from that of humans. He is absolutely dependable; he is generous; he is always right and true.

7. Within the confines of his character, God is endlessly free and creative. He can constantly do new things that have never occurred before.

8. There is nothing beyond God. He is the absolute power, but he is profoundly personal.

9. Since God is not a part of the cosmos, magic and sorcery are radically prohibited. God cannot be manipulated by manipulating the cosmos. Rather, he can only be related to through trust in his revealed promises and by radical surrender to his revealed will.

10. Although God is referred to in exclusively male terms, he is supra-sexual. Sexuality is a feature of the creation, not of ultimate reality. Thus, sexual activity is forbidden in religious practices.

11. This world is profoundly real. Decisions and actions taken here are of genuine significance. They are not merely reflections of events in the invisible world.

12. Since there is only one God, and since he made the world as an expression of his personal will, the creation has a purpose and a goal. This means that it becomes possible to distinguish the present from the past, and the future from the present in terms of the achievement, or non-achievement of those goals. Existence is no longer to be viewed in a circular fashion.

13. There is a single standard of ethics for all the world, and one's ethical behavior is the truest indication of one's relationship to God. Ethical behavior is profoundly religious in character.

14. Religion is a means of expressing trust in God's promises and surrender to his will. Ritual is intended to symbolize this trust and surrender. It does not strengthen cosmic Good or weaken cosmic Evil, since these forces have no independent existence. The attempt to use ritual in a magical way is strictly forbidden. An important aspect of religious behavior is the rehearsal of what God has done and said in unique occurrences with unique persons in time and space.

15. Humans are understood to be the very highest order of God's creation. They are made to be the lords and ladies of creation, functioning in obedient partnership with God. As such, each person has significance, precisely as they differ from the norm. Humans have real freedom to make genuine choices, and they are held accountable for the effects of their choices.

Here then was God's dilemma. His people had been immersed in an understanding that was not merely mistaken, but was perversely wrong at every important point. All of the popular religious forms of the day were permeated with this view. The religious literature of the day was inseparable from it. So God had to go completely outside of it into some form which would be intelligible to people of that day, and yet could somehow be separated from that corrupt understanding.

The covenant was ideal for that purpose. To be sure, the typical form of the covenant between a great king and a vassal people showed the taint of the dominant world view, in that the gods were called upon as witnesses to the covenant. But that part could be altered, as we will see below, and the rest of the form was very adaptable to what God was trying to reveal of this other understanding of reality. In particular, it allowed the Israelites to learn this new understanding by living it out. Suppose God had come to them with the kind of abstract list that I have just given. It would have been largely meaningless. They were a nation of slaves, denied the possibility of education and the leisure of complex thought. Furthermore, the experience of life, apart from divine revelation, is very supportive of the non-Biblical understanding. How are we to understand ultimate reality, anyway? Surely it is by analogy with the world around us. If there are many elements in the cosmos, there must be many gods corresponding to them. If humans are kindly and cruel at the same time, so must the gods be. If we are mastered by sexual desire, so must the gods be, etc., etc. In those kinds of circumstances God had no choice but to find some device whereby his people could learn the true nature of reality by living it out. The covenant form was admirably suited for this purpose.

For instance, the Hittite emperors typically demanded that the subject people recognize no other king than themselves. What a fine way to begin to teach the truth of monotheism. There is no philosophical argument for the superiority of monotheism over polytheism, an argument that would be complex at best. No, if these people wished to be in a relationship with God, they could not recognize any other deity. Thus, they were called to be practical monotheists. Eventually, they would come to realize that there *were* no other gods. Other spirits perhaps, but none on a par with the one God.

Similarly, the covenant form between a great king and a subject people began with a brief historical prologue that explained the historical circumstances that had led up to the making of this covenant. Again, this was a ready made opportunity for God to establish that issues here on earth grow out of the decisions and actions which take place here on earth and not as a result of supposedly "real" actions which have taken place in the invisible world of the divine.

The importance of human history was further underlined by the principal alteration which the Bible makes to the covenant form. At a certain point, after the stipulations had been enumerated, and provisions for the care of the document and its regular reading had been attended to, a whole list of gods were called upon to witness the agreement which had been entered into. Not only were they to witness the covenant, they were also to bless those who obeyed it and curse those who disobeyed it. Obviously, those features could not be duplicated in the Biblical covenant. Exodus 24 tells us what was done in their place. Moses erected twelve pillars, one for each tribe. These became historical markers. They reminded the people that at a certain time in a certain place they had made a decision whose consequences would change them forevermore. And these stones were witnesses to that fact. It was not that the real activity was taking place in the invisible world of the gods. No, it was taking place here in a unique and unrepeatable series of events.

Furthermore, while the bulk of the covenant was made up of the stipulations to which the people had agreed, there was also a place where the king committed himself to do certain things for his people. Here was an opportunity for God to do an unheard of thing: commit himself to his people—upon pain of death! What god would ever do a thing like that? The benefit of being a deity was that you could treat your worshippers however you liked. To voluntarily bind yourself to your people was to suggest that there was something lacking in your understanding of the prerogatives of deity, or that perhaps you were a different kind of deity.

Finally, because the agreement was with a single king, the stipulations could be of an absolute nature. He could say to these people, "If you are going to be in covenant with me, you will *never* do such and such." As seen above, absolute ethics are an impossibility in a polytheistic environment. The gods have too many competing desires. But if there really is only one King to whom we owe allegiance, then absolute ethics of the sort found in the opening summary of the covenant stipulations in Exodus 20 become a possibility.

An interesting feature of the stipulations in the Hittite covenant, especially the absolute ones ("You *shall...*" or "You *shall not...*") is that they seem to represent the personal wishes of the king making the covenant. This becomes apparent when we recognize that the stipulations vary from king to king, but that the different covenants made by the same king frequently show the same or similar stipulations. For instance, the covenants made by the king Shuppiluluma all prohibit adultery. We can conclude from them that this king was personally opposed to this practice. Thus, the covenant reveals something about the preferences of the king and that permits us to infer some things about his character. So it is with God; the kinds of things which he requires his people to do or not to do tell us a great deal about his character.

The Covenant and the Holiness of God

So what does the covenant reveal to us about the character of God? Above everything else that character is described in the word "holy." It is the word that begins the exodus experience in Exodus 3, and it is the word that ends it in Joshua 5. And all along the way, it crops up again and again. The God who makes the covenant, whatever else he may be, is supremely holy. And one of the functions of the covenant is to make that fact crystal clear to the Israelites. But what does the word mean? Interestingly, although the word and its derivatives occur more than 835 times in the Old Testament[1], it is by no means equally as common in the other Semitic languages of the neighboring peoples. To be sure, the cognates occur in several of the languages, such as Akkadian, Arabic, Aramaic and Ugaritic. In these languages, the word refers to that which pertains to a god, distinguishing it from whatever does not pertain to the divine. So from time to time we hear of the gods being described as holy, or of their priests as holy, or of temple vessels as holy, all to say that there is a distinction between the gods and what pertains to them and the rest

---

[1] E. Jenni, *Theologisches Handworterbuch zum Alten Testament*, Bd II, Munich: Kaiser Verlag, 1976, p. 594.

of the cosmos. So holiness speaks of the essence of deity, and of the strange, or different, or even fearful qualities of the unseen world. It may also refer to something that belongs to a deity.

But "holy" is not used in the cognate languages to describe the ethical character of the deities. How could it? For the ethics of the gods were as varied as the number of the gods. So holy El might be beneficent and kindly, while Baal might be domineering and demanding. Anat might be as unpredictable as the weather and Yam as deadly as death. You could say of them all that they were holy in that they were not human. Or you could say of them that they were holy in that they were strange, frightening, and different. But you could not talk about a holy character, or about a holy behavior in regard to them because there was no single god whose character defined the term.

This fact is graphically demonstrated in the Old Testament. There is only one group of people in that collection whose title has the word "holy" in it. With what we know of the Old Testament teachings on holiness, it is perhaps the last group we would expect to bear the title. What is the group? It is the pagan cult prostitutes! They are called the *qadishot*, the "holy women." "How can this be?" we ask. Surely they are the people whose behavior least conforms to God's expectations of holiness. Of course, these women are not conforming to God's expectations, but their name reflects the understanding of the term in paganism. Their "holiness" had nothing to do with their moral behavior, for in the pagan world holiness had nothing to do with moral behavior. These were holy women, as prostitutes are still holy women in India, because they belonged to the gods. Sex, being representative of the life force, is a divine activity and so prostitution everywhere, except in countries influenced by the Old Testament, has been and is controlled by the Temples.

But the Old Testament understanding of holiness, while it begins where its neighbors' understandings do, takes the concept far beyond anything those neighbors ever dreamed of. Yes, in the Old Testament "holy" describes the awesome, terrifying otherness of God. Moses did not have to be told twice to take off his shoes because they were covered with common dirt and the dirt around the burning bush was anything but common. I suspect he could not get those sandals off fast enough. He was in the presence of God! Not only was the bush not consumed, but out of it came a voice, calling his name!

But if this is the place where Israel's neighbors' concept of "holy" starts, it is also the place where it stops. The pagan mind recognizes that there are forces around us that defy our common experiences and call us to awe, wonder, and fear, even to submission. Rudolf Otto, in his well-known book *The Idea of the Holy*,[2] called this the experience of the "Mysterium Tremendum." But this is only the beginning point of the Old Testament understanding. Starting where their neighbors ended, the Hebrews took the concept far beyond anything to be found around them. What happened?

In a word, the covenant happened. What God revealed to the Israelites in the context of the covenant was to revolutionize their entire understanding of deity and of the divine nature. Of course God was holy. They did not need the covenant to teach them that. If this being who called Abraham from Ur of the Chaldees was other than human, then he was holy, by definition. Gods are holy. But in the covenant God began to teach His people that He is the *only* being in existence of whom that term may be justly used. The plagues in Egypt started the process. The Hebrew people were forced to ask if those forces that the Egyptians worshipped, and whom the Lord so handily defeated, really were gods. Was the Nile a goddess? Was the Frog a god? Were the Dung Beetles and the Flies gods? Was Amon the Bull a god? Was Osiris the Vegetation a god? Was Re the Sun a god? Did any of those things have the right to stand on the same level as God and be called "holy"? No. They were not "other" than the world. They were all part of the world. Only that which is truly "other" has a right to be called holy. This recognition that the gods are not really other than this world was carried on by the prophets. Can you use one half of a log to cook your supper, and carve an image from the other half, plate it with gold, put it on a god-shelf, and call that "holy" (see Isaiah 44:9-20; Jer. 10:1-10)? Never!

---

[2] R. Otto, *The Idea of the Holy*, 2nd ed., Oxford: Oxford Univ. Press, 1950, pp. 12ff.

The conclusion that the forces called gods were not really holy was furthered by Yahweh's insistence in the covenant that none of those other beings could even be recognized by the Hebrews (Ex. 20:3). It was pushed still further by the experiences at Sinai and in the wilderness wandering where God's unique otherness from this world and from the gods became absolutely clear. Finally Moses could declare flatly that there is no other God but Yahweh (Deut. 4:35, 39; 32:39). Thus there is only one being in the universe who can properly be called holy. If that is so, then there is only one divine character, and if that character is consistent with itself, then "holy"—that which pertains to the divine—can also describe the divine character. And that is precisely what the covenant serves to do. In the kinds of commands that the Lord lays upon his people we see who he is in his moral character. The nature and details of that character will be the subject of the next chapter.

2

God's Holy Character as Seen in the Covenant

Why did God bring the Hebrew people to the foot of Sinai and enter into the covenant with them? At first glance, it would appear that his sole purpose in delivering them from Egypt was to fulfill his promise to Abraham to make him a great nation and to give that nation a homeland. Looked at in that way, Sinai seems like a rather unnecessary detour.

But what was God's purpose in revealing Himself to Abraham in the first place? And could that purpose be realized simply by taking Abraham's descendants from Egypt into the promised land? In order to answer those questions we need to look at the Abrahamic covenant again. Why does God offer himself and his covenant to Abram? Does he simply want to give Abram a posterity and a bit of land? No, he is addressing a much deeper problem. To be sure, what he *does* offer to Abram is related to that deeper problem, but the offers are addressing the symptoms of the problem and not the problem itself. What is the problem? It is death and the sense of impermanence which death has brought upon our race. Everything we do is made meaningless by the stark fact that one day we will die. That sense of impermanence is multiplied for those who are childless and landless, as Abram and Sarai were. In particular for persons such as these, death seems to mock anything they might do. In the end they will disappear from the face of the earth, and it will be as if they had never lived. On the other hand, if you know that your children will live on after you, and if you

21

have a place of your own which can be shaped and improved and which will remain when you are gone, death is not quite so terrible.

But the provisions of children and a homeland do not solve the problem. They only mitigate some of its most obvious effects. For death is death, and it still makes a mockery of all our attainments. Is there nothing that can be done about death itself? Yes there is, and this is God's ultimate goal in God's offering of himself to Abraham and his descendants. Whence comes death with its transience and impermanence? Genesis 3 tells us that it is the result of that alienation from God which sin brought about. Thus, if death is to be defeated, there must be some means of restored fellowship with our holy Creator. The innateness of that understanding in the human mind is indicated immediately at the beginning of Genesis 4 as it reports the efforts of Cain and Abel, the first generation after the fall of the race, groping in ignorance for a way to restore that fellowship through sacrifices. But since God is transcendent, there is no way for humans to bridge the gulf between Him and themselves. If there is to be a bridge, it must be extended from the Godward side of the gulf.

So God's ultimate purpose for Israel is not that they should have the Promised Land, as important as that symbol is. His purpose is that they should be brought into a relationship with him whereby he could live in their midst and his holiness would not destroy them. That is what he really wants to do for Israel and for all of us. This then, is the point of the detour to Mt. Horeb, or Mt. Sinai. There in that place where God had first revealed his holiness to Moses, and where he had begun to reveal the content of that holiness, he now wishes to reveal his holiness to the whole people and give a further revelation of his holy character. Here he will show what it is going to take for these people, and all people, to enjoy his life-giving presence.

Grace

The first thing that we learn about God's character in the context of the covenant is his grace. Long before the Sinai Covenant this grace is seen in the covenant with Noah. If it is true that Noah was indeed a righteous man with behavior which was perfectly unblemished (Gen. 6:9), it is also true that the same corruption was lying dormant in him which was to be found in all the rest of Adam and Eve's children. It was not because of Noah's deserts that he and his family were saved from the flood. God entered into a covenant with Noah because of his own gracious character (Gen. 6:8). That grace was further extended to the whole world after the flood when God unilaterally declared that he would not destroy the world by means of a flood again.

Again God's grace is the first prominent feature which is seen in the covenant with Abraham. Perhaps the most striking aspect of the Abraham narrative is the recurrence of divine promises, promises in which God freely binds himself to Abraham again and again without any initiation on Abraham's part (see Gen. 12:1-3, 7; 13:14-17; 15:1, 5, 18-20; 17:1-8, 15-16; 22:15-18). The all-but-incredible nature of this grace is made plain in the vision given to Abraham and recorded in Genesis 15. Abraham has believed God's promise that he will give Abraham more descendants than stars in the sky or sand on the seashore (15:6). Then God seals that promise with a vision. He commands Abraham to slaughter certain birds and animals and to divide their carcasses in half. Then Abraham falls into a deep sleep in which horror comes upon him. He is in the presence of the "Mysterium Tremendum." This is confirmed by the symbols of holiness which Abraham sees in his vision: an incense censer and a torch. But what does this Holy One do? He passes between the pieces of the animals. What is the significance of that action? When persons wished to seal a covenant they walked between the halves of a sacrificed animal's body and asked God to do the same thing to them if they ever broke the covenant (cf. Jer. 34:19). That is what God was doing here. He was committing himself to Abraham with the most binding oath possible. He was cursing himself by himself if he should ever fail to keep this promise! Although the writer to the Hebrews is specifically referring to Gen. 22:17 in Hebrews 6:13, his comment that God swore by himself—there being none higher—is equally appropriate to this incident.

Certainly here the astounding nature of God's grace is made evident. What kind of a God is this who would voluntarily bind himself to this man? And why make these promises anyway? What had Abraham ever done for God? Nothing! Yet, God of his own free will offers Abraham those gifts (very unspiritual gifts, by the way—land, a baby, and a lasting reputation) for which Abraham longed. Whatever else these covenant actions say, they tell us of a God who is different from all the other so-called gods. This God gives himself to those by whom he wishes to be worshipped before he asks anything from them.

The same principle may be observed in the Sinai Covenant. It has been common in some quarters of the Christian Church since earliest days to suggest that it was not until New Testament times that the concept of salvation by grace entered religious thought. Such an idea can only be maintained on the basis of a very superficial reading of the Old Testament. Did God appear to his people in Egypt and offer to save them if they would keep the law perfectly for a few hundred years? He did not. He appeared to them in the person of Moses and invited them to enter into the experience of deliverance. They did not have to do anything except believe the promises and act upon them. The Hebrew people were saved from Egyptian bondage by the grace of God and nothing else. Furthermore, that grace could only be received if they acted in faith in the promises of God. The means of salvation was the same in the Old Testament as in the New: by grace through faith.

To be sure, the Judaism that began to emerge after the exile misunderstood this. These survivors of the exile knew that their ancestors had disregarded God's commands, and as a result, had experienced the horror of the exile. These descendants were not going to let that happen again. So they plunged straight from the ditch of license into the ditch of legalism. They began to teach that the means of access to God was acts of righteousness. But this is not what the Old Testament teaches. The Old Testament teaches that we are saved by God's grace alone.

This truth that an essential aspect of God's holy character is grace is underlined in the well-known experience of Moses recorded in

Exodus 3. In many ways, the episode of the Burning Bush is the beginning of the story of the Sinai Covenant. To be sure, the accounts of Moses' birth, of the preservation of his life at the hand of the Egyptian princess, and of the years in the wilderness give us essential background elements. But the story itself begins here. I believe that it is not accidental that the story begins with a theophany, a manifestation of the presence of God, in which holiness is a central feature. This covenant and the experiences surrounding it would demonstrate above all that there is only one being in the universe who can rightfully be called holy. And furthermore, this covenant would demonstrate that it was as much God's character which distinguishes him from his creatures— marks him as Holy—as it is his essence.[3]

As we noted above, this was first of all an experience of the awesome otherness of God for Moses. He recognized that he was in the presence of a whole different order of being from himself. And the very presence of that Being meant that the soil around the bush was of a different order from the soil elsewhere. But what was revealed in this experience was not primarily a matter of God's essence. The words which God speaks in this vision of holiness say nothing of God' mysterious essence. Rather, they speak entirely of God's character in relation to humans. God defines his holiness in terms of his character. He says three things about himself. First, he identifies himself as the God who had revealed himself in gracious promises to Abraham, Isaac and Jacob. Second, he declares that he is sensitive to his people's suffering. And third, he announces that he intends to deliver his people through Moses, thus fulfilling the ancient promises. What do these have to do with "Mysterium Tremendum"? What do they have to do with the holiness which God was at such pains to impress upon Moses? And why does God begin the Sinai Covenant account in this way?

In fact, God is now beginning to make explicit what was implicit in

---

[3]Note that this is the first time "holy" appears in the Bible. Furthermore, there are only four previous occurrences of derivative forms of the root: in Gen. 2:3 where God is said to have "sanctified" the Sabbath, and in Gen. 38:21-22 where Tamar is referred to as a "cult prostitute."

the Noachic and Abrahamic covenants. God is not one of the gods. He is the *only* Holy One, and in him and in his character we see what holiness really consists of. What really distinguishes God from the rest of his creation is a matter of character, a holy character which is as different from that of the gods as day is from night. That difference, as we have already begun to see, is especially made clear in the context of covenant. What is holiness? It is grace, the grace of a Divine Being who offers himself to Abraham, Isaac, and Jacob in undeserved promises of blessing. It is grace, the grace of One who is sensitive to the suffering of human beings. It is grace, the grace of One who is determined to keep his promises to his people in spite of their fear and unbelief.

This is the significance of the Burning Bush episode as the inaugural incident of the Exodus events. These events will demonstrate that there is only one being worthy of the appellation "holy." But they will also demonstrate the full meaning of that term, especially in relation to grace.

It is significant that something of the same sort as happened in Genesis 15 also happened in the context of the Sinai Covenant. In Exodus 24 we read of the sealing of the covenant. Moses recites the terms of the covenant to the people and asks whether they intend to keep those terms. They answer that they will. Moses then writes down the terms in a book. His next step is to erect the pillars of witness. Then he sacrifices oxen and divides the blood in half. One half is thrown on the altar. Then he reads the terms of the covenant to the people and asks if they are still agreeing to those terms. Then he throws the other half of the blood on the people, saying, "Behold the blood of the covenant." What's going on here?

Once again we have a form of the oath ceremony. God and the people are symbolically walking through between the halves of the sacrificial animals. The people are calling down death upon themselves if they ever break any of these stipulations. But notice that God did it first. When half the blood was splashed upon the altar, God was again saying, as he had to Abraham some 600 years earlier, "May I, God, strike myself dead if I ever fail to fulfill one of the terms of this commitment that I am making with you." This is grace! God is committing himself to a group of people for their good, and he does so freely and in advance, not demanding that they prove themselves first.

So what does the covenant teach us about the holiness of God? From beginning to end it teaches us that to be holy is to be gracious.

Ethical Righteousness

If the giving of the covenant is primarily an expression of the grace of God, its content demonstrates the ethical character of God. That is, he treats persons in ways that are first of all consistent with their needs, and only secondarily with his. As was said above, the stipulations of a covenant give an insight into the personal character and preferences of the great king making the covenant. When we look at the Sinai Covenant and at the revelation of God's character that it gives, we recognize that God cares profoundly how humans are treated. When this character is compared to that of the gods, the difference is almost shocking.

Think about the situation: the people have been called upon to accept an exclusive relationship with a holy God. So God addresses the Israelites, *after he has graciously delivered them*, and invites them to enter into a relationship with him wherein he would be their God, and they would be his people (Ex. 19:3-6). They, of course, think this will be a great thing and are glad to accept. After all, they have seen what God has done to the Egyptian gods and to the sea and to the Amalekites. To have a God like that as one's own would certainly be of great benefit! It is at this point that God offers the covenant. Why does he do this? As was said above, it is because God wants us to be in a life-giving relationship with him. But if two parties are to live together, they must agree to certain ground rules, so that the needs of each are met and so that the rights of each are guaranteed. At the same time, it is important that both parties will understand very clearly just what it is that the other wants and needs. This is what the covenant does. In the context of a gracious relationship it shows Israel exactly who God is and what he is like. As was said in chapter 2, it becomes an opportunity to learn by doing. As the Hebrews seek to live out their covenant with God, they are learning who he really is and also what is really true about the universe he created.

So what does the covenant content reveal about God's character? In particular, it reveals his ethical quality. Think for a moment about the covenant content. In order to do so we must look at the entire block of material between Exodus 19 and Numbers 10. In this case the division of the Pentateuch into books does us a disservice because it tends to make us overlook the single thread of thought which runs through this section. The fact that we are intended to read the whole section together is shown by the time references in Numbers 1:1 and 10:11. These are the first time references since 19:1 (in the third month [after the Exodus]) and they tell us that the materials between 19:1 and 10:11 cover the eleven months when Israel was camped at the foot of Sinai.[4] When we look at the material as a single unit bracketed by the time references, we gain a greatly-enhanced understanding of the ethical quality of holiness.

There are five subsections in the unit. The first is "The Book of the Covenant" (Ex. 19-24), in which God outlines the basic terms of the relationship between himself and Israel. The second is the account of the Tabernacle (Ex. 25-40, with the story of the Golden Calf dividing it in two). The third subsection is "The Manual of Worship" (Lev. 1-17), which includes stipulations for sacrifices (1-7), the ordination of priests (8-9), and the ritual of atonement (16-17). Between chapters 9 and 16 is a very important parenthesis that we will return to in a moment. That it is a parenthesis is shown by 16:1 which explicitly picks up where 10:3 leaves off. The fourth sub-section is known as "The Holiness Code" (Lev. 18-27). In these chapters the stipulations of the covenant are reviewed and expanded upon, with the continual refrain that these things must be done because the Lord is holy and because his people must be holy too. The final subsection contains the

---

[4]Exod. 19:1 says they arrived at Sinai at the beginning of the third month after the Exodus. Numbers 1:1 dates the command to take the census on the first day of the second month of the second year, and Num. 10:11 says they left Sinai on the twentieth day of the second month of the second year.

preparations for departure (Num. 1-10:11), with a special focus on the dedication of the Tabernacle and the observance of the Passover.[5]

Now what is the significance of this organization? First of all, it tells us that the reason God gave the people the covenant was so that he might live in their midst. This is why the account of the Tabernacle follows the Book of the Covenant. The people were called upon to live lives like God's, so that they could experience his presence among them. This is why the Golden Calf episode was so tragic. The people knew that they needed God among them, but they thought they could procure his presence for themselves through sympathetic magic—through their own manipulation of the cosmos. The great irony is that at the very time they are trying to do this, God is giving instructions for meeting that need in ways which will be far more wonderful and impressive than their little efforts.

But how can sinful people live in the presence of a Holy God, especially since he is so much more than merely one more of the gods? The answer is the sacrificial system (Lev. 1-17), which follows immediately after the Tabernacle section. Notice very carefully that the sacrifices are not for those who intentionally sin and later think better of it. Neither are they for those who want to enter into a relationship with God. No, the sacrificial system is for those who are already in a relationship with God, those who are committed to living a life like his, and who are enjoying a sense of his presence with them. This is why we have the order: Exodus, Covenant, Tabernacle, Sacrifices and Priesthood. God loves us and wants to live with us, but that is not possible without *continuous* atonement. Otherwise, the purity of his perfection would melt us as the noonday sun melts butter. And note that it is he who determines the terms of what is acceptable and what is not acceptable for us to exist in his presence.

---

[5]Notice that the materials are not necessarily given in the order they were received from God. Num. 7:1 refers to the same events as Exod. 40:16ff. Thus, the materials of Leviticus were given before the Tabernacle was set up, perhaps in the months while it was being constructed. It is also entirely possible that what is now Leviticus was given to Moses during the 40 days on the mountain, when he received the instructions for the Tabernacle. This means that the materials are now in order of their theological significance and not in chronological order.

The climax of the section on Sacrifice and Priesthood is Lev. 16 and 17 — Blood Atonement. Here we finally receive the explanation as to why Abel's sacrifice was acceptable to God, and Cain's was not. There is no forgiveness of sin without the shedding of blood (Heb. 9:22; cf. Lev. 17:11). Unless God makes continual provision for our sin, known and unknown, we will be destroyed by his perfect holiness. Fellowship with God rests forever upon God's provision of atonement.

This last sentence explains the parenthesis between chapters 9 and 16. These chapters function to reinforce our understanding that God is a holy God with whom we may not trifle. The unit begins with the tragic story of Nadab and Abihu, Aaron's sons (10:1-20), and follows on with some apparently unrelated chapters on distinctions between clean and unclean (11:1-15:32). In fact, I believe chapters 10-15 are a closely integrated piece that serves a very important function in the overall structure. What was Nadab and Abihu's problem? Clearly, they did not believe God was really holy. After all, they had been ordained (ch. 9); they were professionals now. They could determine for themselves what was acceptable fire and what was unacceptable fire. And after all, fire was fire, wasn't it? That this was their problem is confirmed by God's comment to Moses: "Among those who come near me I will show myself holy, and before all the people I will be glorified" (Lev. 10:3).

In the pagan view the gods, though holy, are still a part of this world. Therefore, it is possible to manipulate the gods through this world and through priestcraft. Like Aaron who made the Golden Calf, Aaron's sons still believed that God could be approached through human discovery of, and manipulation of, cosmic principles. That is the point, then, of the seemingly petty and arcane commandments concerning the clean and the unclean which appear in chapters 11-15 of Leviticus. How could God convince his people that there really are boundaries in the cosmos, that he is truly other than creation? For there is a boundary between God and human, there is a boundary between human and nature, and there is a boundary between good and evil. (They are not two sides of one coin.) This was especially difficult to convey when all the world around believed the opposite.

So God decreed that whenever a Hebrew sat down to eat, he must ask a question of distinctions concerning his food. It was either clean or unclean, and it was never both at the same time. It either was, or it wasn't. In the same way, death and everything tending toward it or associated with it was unclean. This included disease of various sorts, mold, decay, and hemorrhages of blood or other bodily fluids. There is a distinction between life and death. Nadab and Abihu didn't think there were any distinctions in the world. They thought one could be holy and unholy at the same time. Through these distinctions introduced into everyday life, God was trying to teach the opposite.

Finally, in chapters 18-27, we come to what is called "The Holiness Code." What must God's people be if they were to live in covenant with him and enjoy his intimate presence? They must be holy! Over and over in this section we read those words which Peter quoted, "You must be holy, for I am holy." That this is the capstone idea of the entire section from Exodus 19 onward is shown by its introduction in Exodus 19:6 where God tells Israel that the effect of their accepting the covenant will be that the entire nation will become holy. Here in "The Holiness Code" that introductory statement is fleshed out in great detail.

But what does this mean? How can we possibly be holy as God is holy? Are we all to become gods, other than human? Well, that might be thought possible in the world-view where the gods are continuous with the cosmos. But it is certainly not a possibility in the biblical worldview where God is emphatically not continuous with his creation; where he radically transcends it. But perhaps it simply means what it means elsewhere in the ancient world: a person or a thing associated with a god becomes holy (off-limits for ordinary use). Thus for God's people to be holy would simply mean that they belong exclusively to him and it would not necessarily have behavioral implications at all.

But that is emphatically not the case here, and in fact, it was not the case in paganism either. For being holy to a god did have behavioral implications. It was precisely because the cult prostitute was holy to his or her god that he or she engaged in promiscuous sexual behavior.

Why did they do it? Because that is what their god or goddess did. Those prostitutes could no more decide to be chaste than a bird could decide not to fly. To belong to a god exclusively does have behavioral implications.

But even if that were not the case in the world around Israel, the data here would make it plain in any case. It is precisely in the context of human behavior that God calls for his people to demonstrate their holiness. Furthermore, these are commands. If holiness was an automatic result of being brought into an exclusive relation with a holy God, then as soon as the covenant was sealed in Exodus 24, the nation would be holy and no more commands would be needed. But that is clearly not the case. The people are in an exclusive relationship with God, and yet they are commanded to become holy.

As an example of the behavioral nature of being holy, look at Leviticus 19. What does it mean to be holy as God is holy? We might expect that it would involve praying a lot, or giving a lot of sacrifices, or fasting, or spending a lot of time at the Tabernacle in holy convocations, or in other obviously religious behaviors. In fact, those kinds of behaviors are mentioned in this section of Leviticus, but they are by no means in the majority. If we look at this chapter as representative, we discover that to be holy as God is holy is to honor your father and mother, and to keep the Sabbath (v. 3). It is to avoid idol worship (v. 4). It is to eat the peace offering while it is fresh (vv. 5-8). It is to leave some of the harvest for the poor (vv. 9-10). It is not to steal, or lie, or to swear to do something that you cannot or will not do (vv. 11-12). It is not to enrich yourself through fraud or through unfair treatment of those who work for you (v. 13). It is to treat the handicapped with kindness (v. 14). It is to treat all people, rich or poor, justly (v. 15). It is to have nothing to do with slander or gossip (v. 16). It is to love your neighbor as yourself, refusing to bear a grudge, and being willing to correct him when he is wrong (vv. 17-18). It is to maintain distinctions between kinds of animals, kinds of seeds and kinds of cloth (v. 19). It is to refrain from sexual relations with another man's slave (vv. 20-22). It is to allow fruit trees time to propagate themselves (vv. 23-25). It is to avoid pagan practices, such as eating blood, cutting the hair in certain ways, gashing or tattooing oneself (vv. 26-28). It is to keep your daughter from prostitution (v. 29). It is to keep the Sabbath and reverence the sanctuary (v. 30). It is to avoid all uses of magic (v. 31). It is to honor the aged (v. 32). It is to love strangers as yourself (vv. 33-34). It is to use honest weights and measures (v. 35-36).

I have summarized this chapter at length to underscore the point: the holiness which God expects of his people is behavioral, and it is a behavior which cuts right across the grain of life, touching every aspect of it, whether personal, social, moral, civil or religious. When God calls his people to be holy as he is holy, he is not merely asking them to live lives exclusively dedicated to him. Neither is he asking them to be especially religious. Rather, he is calling them to share his unique character, one that will alter how they approach every aspect of their lives.

Here then is the goal of salvation: that God's people should be holy, that they should share his character. God delivered Israel from bondage in Egypt so that he could live in their presence and they in his. If that is to happen, then his people must share his character. As Amos says, "Can two walk together unless they be agreed?" (Amos 3:3). Or as John says, "God is light and in Him is no darkness at all. If we claim to have fellowship with Him yet walk in darkness, we lie and do not live by the truth"(1 Jn. 1:6).

The goal of salvation is not that people should be free of physical and spiritual bondage in order to live as they choose. The goal of salvation is fellowship with God within the parameters of his character and nature. This has been God's goal since the tragedy of Genesis 3 and it remains so in the Christian era. The thought that the primary purpose of the Cross is forgiveness is misguided at best.

I want to underline again the point made earlier: the covenant (or, the law) is not the means of entering into a relationship with God, or of receiving his delivering grace. The Israelites had already been delivered when they reached the foot of Sinai. And even though they were not always comfortable with the idea, they were already in a relationship with God. Thus, the covenant was not the way to God;

rather, it was the means of walking with God. At the risk of over-emphasis, let it be said again: holy living is the intended consequence of gracious salvation.

We return now to the main theme of this section: the covenant as a revelation of the ethical character of God. Why does God tell his people that those who belong to him will give honor to their parents, will not lie, will not steal, will not commit adultery, will not murder, and will not covet? What do these have to do with religion? Why does God command them? He commands them so that as the people seek to fulfill these terms of their covenant they are learning something. They are learning that God is not one of the gods. He does not see persons as objects to be used until they are old and then thrown away. He has complete integrity; he does not say one thing and then deny that he said it. He values persons as individuals, thus their property cannot be appropriated for some other use, nor can their lives be taken from them for any self-serving ends. He is absolutely faithful to his promises, and therefore, of all the sexual sins, adultery—breaking faith—is the worst. He is a Spirit and he knows that the acquisition of material things, especially when that acquisition is born out of envy, is to miss the point of living. This is who God is, and its importance is emphasized by the fact that it takes up fully six-tenths of the summary of the covenant stipulations (the Ten Commandments). Those who belong to God must act in these ways because that is the kind of God he is. To live in defiance of these while insisting that one is forgiven is to do the very thing which the Hebrews did and which brought them to destruction and despair. One who is in a relationship with God is expected to be holy and that holiness is manifested in transformed social ethics. The goal of redemption is transformed character, and unless that goal is achieved mere deliverance from a sense of condemnation is misshapen at best and abortive at worst, as it was for the whole generation lost in the wilderness.

Faithfulness

If the giving of the covenant demonstrated that God's holiness is gracious, and if the content of the covenant demonstrated that it is ethical, then the outworking of the covenant demonstrated that holiness is faithful and kind.

As said above, the covenant was sealed with the most serious kinds of oaths. Both God and the people called down death upon themselves if they should ever break the covenant. Thus, when the people broke it in most egregious ways hardly more than a month after they had entered into it, God was entirely just in threatening to destroy them (Ex. 32). If he had burned them all up on the spot, it would have been no more than they had asked for.

Yet it took very little persuasion on Moses' part for God to relent and determine to keep his side of the covenant whether Israel keeps its side or not. In fact, one may ask whether the experience related in Exodus 32 actually describes a test of Moses. Has Moses learned who God really is and what he is really like? Will he step into the gap and call for God to be true to himself whether Israel was true or not? In this regard there are some important similarities with the dialogue between Yahweh and Abraham over the fate of Sodom and Gomorrah in Genesis 19. There, as here, God tells his man what he intends to do in advance—explicitly there, and implicitly here—inviting comment and, indeed, intercession. God will lay aside his just anger on the slightest pretext, as Abraham and Moses discovered, and as Jonah knew very well many years later (Jonah 4:2).

What Moses points out to God is that behind this broken covenant stand God's promises to Abraham, Isaac and Jacob. For God to destroy these people and raise up a new one in the name of Moses would abrogate those promises. And Moses knows enough about God to know that he is not that sort of God. Moses has at least begun to grasp the truth of Exodus 20:5b-6: "...I, the LORD your God am a jealous God, punishing the children for the sin of the fathers to the third and fourth generation of those who hate me, but showing love to a thousand generations who love me and keep my commandments." The Hebrew word translated "love" here is really much more expressive than the English word "love."[6] The problem is that there is

---

[6]It is the word חֶסֶד, "hesed." Although it occurs more than 240 times in the Hebrew Bible, it has no known cognates in other Semitic languages.

no one English word that captures all that the Hebrew word connotes. It connotes the earnest, undeserved, and unexpected generosity of one who does not have to give it. On the lowest level, it can be translated with "kindness." So Boaz thanks Ruth for her "kindness" in choosing him for her husband instead of some more handsome, younger man (Ruth 3:10). On a higher level, it is "God's kindness" which David shows to Mephibosheth, the handicapped son of Jonathan, in giving him a lifetime pension (2 Sam. 9:3). On the highest level, it is the "mercy" of God whereby he does not remember us according to our youthful sins (Psa. 27:5).

What Exodus 20:5b-6 is saying is that while God is indeed just and will bring upon humans the effects of their sins, he will limit those effects to a few generations, even among those who hate him. On the other hand he will extend undeserved generosity to a thousand generations (cf. Deut. 7:9) of those who love him. Moses has begun to understand this and he reminds God of this truth of his character. Should not this God, who is so different from the gods, extend to the descendants of Abraham, Isaac, and Jacob this kind of undeserved generosity? And without further ado God does just that. There is no suggestion here of some raging tyrant whose ego is offended, and of a cowering, but brave hero, who is willing to back the tyrant down until finally, grudgingly, he cools off. Rather, we have here the first in a long series of experiences in which the Hebrews break their covenant again and again while God in kindness, generosity, mercy, grace, and love continues to stand by them, refusing to let go of them.

This is the point that is made with such force in Exodus 34. After what must have been an exceedingly trying experience for Moses (the encounter with God, the discovery of the true extent of Aaron's and the people's apostasy, the calling out of the Levites to kill the ringleaders, the successful pleading with God not to withdraw his presence from them on the rest of the trip to the Promised Land), Moses asks for a sign of God's continued favor. Interestingly, he asks for a vision of God's glory (33:18), but God responds that he will show Moses his goodness (33:19). Moses wanted to see some manifestation of the holy essence, but God wanted him to understand more of the holy character.

Although Moses was permitted to see some visible representation of God (his back), it was not this that impressed him, for there is not one word of description of the vision given. What did impress him was the message about God that he heard proclaimed in the context of the vision. The words were these:

> "The LORD, the LORD, the compassionate and gracious God, slow to anger, abounding in love (hesed) and faithfulness, maintaining love (hesed) to thousands, and forgiving wickedness, rebellion and sin. Yet he does not leave the guilty unpunished; he punishes the children and their children for the sin of the fathers to the third and the fourth generation"(Ex. 34:6b-7).

And throughout the Old Testament when the Israelites describe God, it is always in these terms (cf. Num. 14:18; Deut. 4:31; Neh. 9:17; Ps. 103:3-4; Joel 2:13; Jonah 4:2). When we ask the Israelite people what their God is like, they do not, as some Christians would expect, speak of him as a God of wrath. Instead they tell us of a God of incredible patience, who extends undeserved generosity to thousands of those who love him and keep his commandments. It is as though they say to us, "It is not surprising that God got angry at us. We broke our covenant, the one in which we called down death on ourselves, a thousand times. What is surprising is that God would not give up on us. He continued to hold us, to believe in us, to hope for us, to invite us to start over again. He kept his side of the covenant when there was no earthly reason whatsoever to do so."

So the covenant, which revealed the holy character of God, revealed that his otherness was not merely in grace, nor in ethical uprightness, but also in undeserved and unexpected faithfulness. Very frequently, the word *hesed* is accompanied by the word *'emet*, "truth."[7] This word

---

[7]The two words occur together some 33 times. Of these 20 have to do with the character of God. They are: Gen. 24:27; 32:10; Exod. 34:6; 2 Sam. 2:6; Pss. 25:10; 40:10, 11; 57:3, 10; 61:7; 69:13; 85:10; 86:15; 89:14; 108:4; 115:1; 117:2; 138:2; Isa. 16:5 (Messiah); Mic. 7:20.

reinforces the sense of faithful love which *hesed* connotes, because it contains the idea of relational dependability. God is "true" in that he is absolutely reliable. He will do what he has said he would, even when he no longer has to, or even when it might be to his own disadvantage. Thus God is "true" to his word, and he is true to people. Since this God is the sole creator of the world, this idea must of necessity lead to the concept of "truth," the idea that there is that in God's world which is "true" apart from any subjective perception of it. As is being proven in Western society today, the idea of "truth" is untenable apart from the recognition that there is one transcendent, faithful Creator of the world.

What then is the purpose of God's covenants, particularly the Sinai Covenant? Its purpose is really four-fold, and we have now considered the first three of those. They are: First, the covenant is intended to reveal the true nature of reality, beginning with Yahweh's sole lordship and his transcendence and continuing through the incredible worth of humans. Second, by making a covenant with his people God seeks to reveal his holy character. And third, he seeks to show what his intent for human life is. In many ways the covenant accomplishes these three purposes simultaneously. That is, it calls humans into an exclusive relationship with God in which they are expected to live lives that are consistent with his. As they seek to fulfill these covenant terms, they slowly come to realize the amazing qualities of God which underlie all reality; qualities which they might agree to if they were simply told them, but ones whose amazing character they would never appreciate until they sought to live them. At the same time, they are beginning to experience God's ultimate goal for us humans: that we should live in fellowship with him sharing his ethical character.

3

The Covenant and Human Nature

We turn now to the fourth purpose of the covenant in the Old Testament. Not only was it intended to reveal the character of God and what his intention is for human life. It was also intended to reveal the human character. As Paul says, it was to be a schoolmaster to bring us to Christ. It was not intended to be a means whereby humans could make themselves acceptable to God. Neither was it to be a ladder whereby greater and greater levels of sainthood could be attained. When the terms of the covenant are used in that way the covenant becomes not a blessing but a curse, as Romans 7 so clearly shows.

But at the outset, this was not at all clear. The terms of the covenant when considered objectively seem to be such commonsensical measures. They seem self-evidently correct and eminently appropriate. Obviously this is the way humans should live, and if they did, life would work. Thus, the Jewish term "Torah" has none of the negative connotations that the English "law" has. "Torah" means "instruction," and that is how the Jew understands the covenant. God has graciously given to the Jewish people the manual on how to live. Unlike "law" which has connotations of limitation of freedom, "Torah" suggests new freedom through using a device as it was intended to be used.

Thus, when Moses first recited, and then read, the terms of the covenant at the foot of Sinai, the people responded with blithe assurance. Of course they would live up to these expectations, rigorous though they seemed. Why not? God had graciously delivered them from Egypt, and now he was offering an exclusive relationship with himself. Furthermore, he had graciously showed them how to live successful lives. Of course they would do all these things. No problem! So it seemed of little consequence to them to call down death upon themselves if they ever broke the covenant. They could not imagine themselves doing such a thing. Little did they know that within little more than a month they would be dancing around a golden idol, praising it for having delivered them from Egypt. No problem? They, as children of Adam and Eve, had a big problem and they did not know it.

It is no different with us. A young convert rises from the altar, face shining. When we ask them what has just occurred in their lives, they give a ringing testimony of Christ's grace accepted, of sins forgiven, of new life begun. There is no question— this person has found Christ and his salvation. And so we ask them, "Are you going to live for Christ." "Oh yes," they respond, "how could I ever do anything else! He died for me! Of course I am going to live for him, and him alone." Are they lying? Are they speaking with their fingers crossed? Not at all. They are as sincere as it is possible to be. But some cynic in the back row says, "We'll see about that." Why does he say that? Because experience has shown us that even with the sincerest intentions, there is something within us that works against our best efforts to live the life of God. The Israelites described this in several ways. Jeremiah says, "The heart is deceitful above all things and beyond cure. Who can understand it?" (17:9). David says, "Surely I was sinful at birth, sinful from the time my mother conceived me" (Ps. 51:5). But perhaps the most expressive of all of these is the one found in Genesis 6:5: "The LORD saw how great man's wickedness on the earth had become, and that *every inclination of the thoughts of his heart was only evil all the time.*" What the Hebrew says is that the very way we go about forming images in our minds is wholly corrupt. It does not take very much reflection to recognize the profundity of this ancient observation. We do not automatically focus upon what is noble, good, and true, as

Paul urged us to do (Phil. 4:8). Rather our imaginations drift to the pornographic, the horrible, the perverse, and the corrupt. We poke fun at literature which consistently presents life in a positive, clean and optimistic light, calling it "unrealistic," or "saccharine." On the other hand, we pay the compliment of careful attention and discussion to anything that focuses on the degraded, seamy aspects of life.

The understanding of the "evil imagination" appears elsewhere in Hebrew in Genesis 8:21 and Deuteronomy 31:21, and it becomes the common way of speaking about sinful human nature in Rabbinic Hebrew. Something has gone wrong in the human heart and mind. If we once were a clean page for God to write upon, it is now no longer the case. We are inclined to do the wrong thing; we are inclined toward death and not toward life, even in the very way we frame our thoughts. And any philosophy or way of life which does not take account of this will founder. All of the great utopian schemes, from Zinzendorf's "Herrnhut" to Marx's Communes, have foundered on this rock. In many ways the entire Enlightenment fell afoul of this truth. The enlightenment thinkers were certain that the human problem was ignorance fostered by the blind dogmatism of tradition and authority. They were certain that if the human spirit could be unshackled by the application of scientific reason, human difficulties would all disappear. Marx and Engels carried this all a step farther. Rejecting the dominant Idealism of the nineteenth century, which thought of human culture in essentially spiritual terms, these two concluded that "spirit" is merely an abstraction, and that matter is what is really significant. Therefore, the human problem is fundamentally economic. If economic equality was at first forcibly maintained, with those who did the work having chief say in how the fruits of their labor was distributed, then true peace and equality would follow in short order.

We are now in a position to say that both of these versions of enlightenment thinking, the earlier in the French Revolution and the later in the Russian Revolution, have failed. The fundamental human problems are neither ignorance nor faulty distribution of wealth, as serious as those problems are, and as worthy as they are of careful attention. Education will not make a person noble, or self-denying, or generous. It simply gives him or her more efficient ways of achieving his or her self-serving ends. Likewise, enforced economic equality does not cause the state to wither away, or to decrease the occurrence of violent oppression. In fact, as time passes both of these, the state and violent oppression, become the more necessary in order to maintain the supposed equality.

No, the Hebrews knew 3000 years before the French Revolution in 1789 that the problems of human civilization are not external, they are internal. And how did they learn this? They did not learn it through philosophical speculation. Instead, they learned it just as they learned the nature of God. They learned it through the medium of the covenant. Thinking it would be easy to serve him in ways in keeping with his character, they blithely entered the covenant with its oaths to be faithful or die. And when they broke it so soon after its sealing, they were sure that this was just an aberration and that it did not signify anything serious. But in fact it did signify such a thing, because they broke it again and again. They broke it at Kadesh-Barnea when they refused to trust God and disobeyed his command to enter the promised land. They broke it when they murmured and complained in the wilderness. They broke it when they worshipped the Midianite gods at Baal-Peor. And these were only the beginning. The whole history of Israel is captured in two motifs: the constant and continuing failure of the mass of Israel to keep the covenant, and the constant and continuing faithfulness of God to Israel through the covenant.

Isaiah represents what Israel had learned about God and itself in poignant words in chapters 63 and 64 of his book:

> I will tell of the kindnesses (*hesed*) of the LORD,
>   the deeds for which he is to be praised,
>   according to all the LORD has done for us—
> yes, the many good things he has done
>   for the house of Israel,
>   according to his compassion
>   and his many kindnesses (*hesed*).

He said, "Surely they are my people,
  sons who will not be false to me";
  and so he became their Saviour.
In all their distress he too was distressed,
  and the angel of his presence saved them.
In his love and mercy he redeemed them;
  he lifted them up and carried them all the days of old.
Yet they rebelled
  and grieved his Holy Spirit.
So he turned and became their enemy
  and he himself fought against them. (63:7-10)

For when you did awesome things that we did not expect,
  you came down, and the mountains
    trembled before you.
Since ancient times no one has heard,
  no ear has perceived,
no eye has seen any God besides you,
  who acts on behalf of those who wait for him.
You come to the help of those who gladly do right,
  who remember your ways.
But when we continued to sin against them,
  you were angry.
  How then can we be saved?
All of us have become like one who is unclean,
  and all our righteous acts are like filthy rags;
we all shrivel up like a leaf,
  and like the wind our sins sweep us away.
No one calls on your name
  or strives to lay hold of you;
for you have hidden your face from us
  and made us waste away because of our sins. (64:3-7)

Although the Hebrew people recognized the essential goodness of
the Torah, they were unable to obey it. There was something within
them that preferred darkness to light, and evil to good. They would
rather have bondage under the illusion of freedom than to have
freedom within the confines of service. Thus the covenant not only

showed the people that they were not like God, but also that there was something in them which did not *want* to be like God.

Thus, if the covenant was intended to make the people of Israel a holy people it failed miserably. They belonged to him, but hardly exclusively. They knew very clearly how he expected them to live, but if we are to believe the prophets, very few of them lived in that manner. Viewed from that perspective the covenant was a colossal failure. But viewed from another perspective, the covenant succeeded wonderfully well. That is, as we have said above, the covenant functioned to reveal four things: the true nature of reality; the holy character of God; God's intention that humans should share his holy character; and the fundamental inability of humans to be holy. In this sense, the covenant was masterfully successful. When we come to the end of the Old Testament story, we know each of these with perfect clarity, and are prepared for the next step in God's plan. But before we go on to consider that next step, we need to address one more issue that this paragraph raises. Does not the considerable failure of Israel to fulfill God's plans for her indicate that he never intended for her to do so, but was simply setting up an impossible standard as a way of showing its impossibility? Was he not showing that objective holiness—a life like his—was quite impossible, and that if we were ever to be holy it would need to be of a forensic sort whereby God declares us holy when in fact we are not?

4

Life Expectations
in the Old Testament

What was it God wanted of his people? Without question, as we have shown in the previous chapters, he wanted a relationship with them. He wanted a restoration of the fellowship that had once existed in the Garden at the dawn of time. This is why the giving of the covenant in the Book of Exodus is followed by the account of the Tabernacle. The most immediate result of the covenant was the possibility of the people's experiencing the presence of God in their midst. And by the same token, the most immediate result of the breaking of the covenant in the Golden Calf episode was the potential removal of God's presence from them. As a result of Moses' intercession, the people are not destroyed and God continues to be willing to give them the promised land, but He says that he cannot go up with them. This occasions even more intense intercession from Moses, who clearly does understand what is at stake here. What good is that promised land without the presence of God? "If your presence does not go with us, do not send us up from here," he says (Exod. 33:15). So the intended purpose of the covenant was fellowship.[8]

---

[8]An interesting confirmation of this is found in 1 John in the opening paragraph. John tells his readers that he has experienced the revelation of God in the Incarnation. He goes on to say that he is telling them about this so that they may share the fellowship which he has with the Father and the Son. In other words, the purpose of revelation is fellowship. (1 John 1:1-4)

But is this all? And furthermore, how is the covenant intended to make this fellowship possible? Again, I have argued above that the placement and content of the book of Leviticus is intended to teach us that fellowship is possible only for those in whom the covenant is producing godly (God-like) character. But does God really expect such character of his people? Especially since most of them so radically failed to manifest it?

The Old Testament evidence argues that the answer to these questions is yes. The covenant stipulations were not merely an impossible obstacle whose purpose was to make the people fail. Apart from the cynical nature of such an approach, a nature that would be strange coming from the holy God, there is clear evidence in the Old Testament text that God really does expect his people to share his character.

This evidence is found in two groupings of concepts revolving around two different words. Both of these concepts were translated in the Authorized Version (AV) with words for perfection along with other words. Later versions continue to translate with words for perfection when the reference is to God or his activity, but have abandoned them when the reference is to humans. This does not indicate a new understanding of the meaning of the text, but rather reflects our current despair over human perfectibility. We do not believe such a thing is possible and are therefore reluctant to translate the Bible in such a way as to make it seem so. The fact that the terms are still translated with words denoting or connoting perfection everywhere but in the case of humans seems to confirm that this is what has happened.

Perfect in the Sense of Whole, Complete, Without Defect

The first concept has to do with that which is complete and without blemish. The Hebrew root underlying the various words is תמם, *tmm*. Five different forms of this root are used to refer to human behavior that is without fault. The AV translates four of these at least once each with forms of the English word "perfect." The first form to be considered is the verb. Most occurrences of the verb have to do with the completion of an object or a process, such as something being totally consumed (cf. Num. 14:35). But there are four places where the verb is used of human behavior, and these show that the kind of completion being talked is of a moral and ethical nature. Job 22:3 has Eliphaz asking Job, "Is it any gain (to God) if you make your ways *perfect?*" Psalm 19:13 says, "Keep back thy servant from presumptuous sins; let them not have dominion over me: then I shall be upright, and I shall be *innocent* from the great transgression." 2 Samuel 22:26 (paralleled by Ps. 18:25) says that "with the *upright* (noun form) you will show yourself upright."

In other words, Job's behavior toward God is not partly obedient and partly disobedient; it is wholly obedient. In the same way, the person who is delivered from insolence will be completely obedient. Rebellion will have no part in his or her life. Likewise, God will respond in an unmixed way to the person whose obedience toward him is unmixed.

This point becomes even more clear in the occurrences of the noun and adjective forms of the root. Perhaps the most significant of these is the adjective *tamim.* This word occurs 91 times in the Hebrew Bible. Of these AV translated 19 with words for perfection. But it is those occurrences which are typically not translated in this way which give us the most help in understanding those which are. Fully 56 occurrences have to do with sacrificial animals. The animals are to be complete in the sense of being utterly unblemished. That is, they are perfect specimens. This is not necessarily to say that they were show animals, but it is to say that there was no defect to be found in them (cf. Exod. 12:5; Lev. 1:3, 10, etc.). Note especially Leviticus 22:21 where *tamim* is explained: "When anyone offers a sacrifice of well-being to the LORD, in fulfillment of a vow or as a freewill offering, from the herd or from the flock, to be acceptable it must be perfect (*tamim*); there shall be no blemish in it" (NRSV). This understanding is further confirmed by the Septuagint, the Greek translation, which usually translates the Hebrew with αμωμοσ, *amomos*, "faultless." [9]

---

[9]The noun *mᵉtom* is used in three of its four occurrences to describe a healthy, or whole ("sound" AV) body (Ps. 38:3, 7; Isa. 1:6).

When this word is applied to God or to his behavior, it provokes little comment. So we read in Deuteronomy 32:4, "He is the Rock, his work is *perfect*," (AV) or in 2 Sam. 22:31 "God, his way is *perfect*." (AV), or in Job 37:16 "…the works of him who is *perfect* in knowledge." (AV), or in Ps. 19:7 "The law of the LORD is *perfect*." (AV) In these instances the modern translations do not differ from AV. But in the next eleven references, these translations very rarely agree with AV. For in these cases it is human character or performance which is being discussed. All the translations given are AV.

> "Noah was a just and *perfect* man." Gen. 6:9
>
> (To Abraham) "Walk before me and be *perfect*." Gen. 17:1
>
> "You shall be *perfect* with the LORD." Deut. 18:13
>
> (David) "God…makes my way *perfect*." 2 Sam. 22:33
>
> (Elihu of himself) "He that is *perfect* in knowledge is
>   with you." Job 36:4
>
> "I will behave myself wisely in a *perfect* way." Ps. 101.2
>
> "He that walks in a *perfect* way, he shall serve me." Ps. 101:6
>
> "The *perfect* will remain." Prov. 2:21
>
> "The righteousness of the *perfect* will direct his way."
>   Prov. 11:5
>
> (To the King of Tyre) "You were *perfect* in all your ways
>   .…until wickedness was found in you." (Ezek. 28:15)

In addition to these statements, we should also note several other occurrences of *tamim* where the AV does not use "perfect," but where a faultless attitude or faultless obedience is clearly intended. The words used are "sincere," "upright," "undefiled" and "sound." Some examples of these are:

> "Now therefore serve the LORD in *sincerity* and in truth:
>   and put away the gods which your fathers served on the
>   other side of the flood, and in Egypt; and serve the
>   LORD." (Josh. 24:14)
>
> "Now therefore, if you have done truly and *sincerely* .…"
>   (Judges 9:16; cf. 9:19)
>
> "I was also *upright* before him, and kept myself from mine
>   iniquity." (2 Sam. 22:24)

"…and with the upright man thou wilt shew thyself *upright.*" (2 Sam. 22:26)

"He that walks *uprightly,* and works righteousness, and speaketh the truth from his heart." (Ps. 15:2)

"Whoso walketh *uprightly* shall be saved: but he that is perverse in his ways shall fall at once." (Prov. 28:18; see also Job 12:4; Pss. 37:18; 84:11; Prov. 11:20; 28:10; Amos 5:10)

"Blessed are the *undefiled* in the way, who walk in the law of the LORD." (Ps. 119:1)

"Let my heart be *sound* in thy statutes; that I be not ashamed." (Ps. 119:80)

The other three noun/adjective forms show much the same thought. The word *tom* occurs 23 times, all but five of which have to do with human behavior. The common AV translations are "integrity" or "uprightness." Thus:

"In the *integrity* of my heart and the innocency of my hands I have done this." (Gen. 20:5)

"Walk before me as David thy father did, in *integrity* of heart, and in uprightness. (1 Kings 9:4)

"I will walk within my house with a *perfect* heart." (Ps. 101:2)

"Better is the poor that walks in his *uprightness,* than he that is perverse in his ways, though he be rich." (Prov. 28:6)

The feminine form of this same noun occurs five times, four of which describe the "integrity" of Job (2:3, 9; 27:5; 31:6). The fifth occurrence is in Proverbs 11:3 where the "integrity" of the upright (the straight, *yasar*) is contrasted with the perversity of transgressors.

The noun *tam* occurs 13 times, ten of which refer to human behavior, with fully seven found in Job. AV translates nine of the ten, and all of those in Job with "perfect." Two of the occurrences that do not describe behavior are helpful because they are the words of the lover in Song of Solomon describing his beloved (Song 5:2; 6:9). That is, she is one whose beauty is complete in every way. Thus, when we are told that Job was a "*perfect* and upright (*yasar*)," man who feared God and rejected evil (1:1, 8; 2:3; see also 8:20; 9:20, 21, 22) we understand that Job's moral and ethical behavior was all that could be expected of a human being.

How shall we understand these kinds of statements that seem to speak of a way of living which is faultless in regard to God and his expectations for human life? What we must not do is to dismiss them or try to explain them away. Clearly the Bible knows of the possibility of unblemished behavior on the part of humans, behavior which is everything which could possibly be expected of us. Noah was such a person, and Abraham was commanded to be, as were the children of Israel. Of special interest is David's statement in 2 Samuel. It is of interest because only two verses before this place where he says that God makes his (David's) way perfect, he has said in the same words that God's way is perfect. In other words, David is bearing testimony that his own behavior is of precisely the same quality as God's. If this troubles us, then we should remember that Jesus calls us to the same thing when He says to us, "You must be perfect as your Father in Heaven is perfect" (Matt. 5:48). These thoughts are continued in both Psalms and Proverbs. We are told that there are persons who can be called "the perfect," and we are told that the requisite for service to God is to walk in a "perfect" way. Anything that obscures these truths does a disservice to all of us.

But what does it mean? How dare David say that his way is as perfect as God's is, even if he gives God the credit for it? David was an adulterer and a liar, a judicial murderer. How dare he say such a thing? How dare Elihu claim to be perfect in knowledge? Who knows everything? But perhaps this is the point at which we can gain entrée to the proper understanding. Elihu contrasts his unblemished knowledge with "falseness." In other words, the emphasis is not upon quantity or extent, but upon quality. Elihu's knowledge is everything that could possibly be expected of it in its integrity of purpose and intent. He is not telling things he knows to be false. He is not showing off artificial mental constructs. He is not playing with words. He is not trying to score off Job and prove that he is more intelligent than his elder. He is speaking out of "perfect" knowledge. It is not corrupted by self-seeking or by deceitfulness.

This is how David can speak of God having perfected David's way. He is not necessarily saying that he does everything right. But he is saying that God has made it possible for him to serve God with complete integrity. He is not serving God for base motives, nor for deceitful ones. He is serving God for God's sake and nothing else. His behavior is thus unblemished. It is all that could be expected of it in terms of its motivation and focus. This of course does not necessarily mean that David knows all the hidden motivations of his heart. Psalm 51 speaks of something of the shock that came to David when he saw the full horror of what he had done with Bathsheba and Uriah. So he pleads for a cleansing which will be deeper than anything he has known before. Something of the same sort appears at the end of Psalm 19 and again at the end of Psalm 139. Thus, a way that is perfect in the sense that it is marked by unblemished devotion and obedience, may not be a way that is necessarily perfect in performance. There may be a hundred and one things that prevent us from performing perfectly, but on the basis of these biblical statements, it is entirely possible for a human to walk perfectly before God. In fact, the Bible says that this is the minimum requirement for those who would serve God.

But perhaps someone will say, "Oh, is that all you mean? You don't really mean perfect. You mean blameless, or with integrity, or something like that. God performs perfectly, but humans don't, so we shouldn't use the same words to describe the activity." But the Bible does! That is, when the Bible speaks of God's perfection in this sense it is not speaking about his performance either! If the Bible calls us to be perfect as God is perfect, using the same words in both places, and if it is perfectly clear that humans cannot perform perfectly, then we are not speaking about God's performance either. We are speaking about the manner in which God performs. He is perfect. That is, He does not operate from deceitful, or self-serving motives, and *neither should we.* Furthermore, we really can live in that way. We really can live above constant self-reference. We really can be delivered from the need to put others down so as to raise ourselves up, etc. This is why the Bible uses the same words to describe God's way and our way. And our translations should reflect the integrity of the original language.

The Perfect Heart

This truth is demonstrated in a similar way by another set of concepts. These concepts are centered on the Hebrew root שׁלם, *slm*, which also, like *tmm*, has to do with completeness. Here, however, the sense does not have to do so much with lack of blemishes as with all parts being present, thus, wholeness. One of the well-known noun forms is *shalom*, that is, a situation, whether physical, emotional, social, or civil, where all the requisite parts are present and functioning harmoniously. Thus, the translation of *shalom* is not only "peace," but "well-being."

Another example that helps us to understand the ideas present in the term has to do with paying a debt. When a debt is unpaid, something is incomplete, unsatisfied. Thus, to pay a debt is to *shillem* it, to complete it, or to pacify it, or in terms somewhat less foreign in English, to satisfy it. Now the transaction is complete, and nothing is left undone; *shalom* is present.

These examples help us to understand the 14 occurrences of the adjective *shalem* where it is used to describe the "heart" of a person. In Hebrew "heart" is an all-inclusive term. While it is used to represent the affections, that is not its primary connotation. The heart is the center of the personality. Thus it refers to the powers of discernment, the will, and the motivations, as well as the affections.[10] It is not primarily the seat of the emotions. Those are resident in the bowels and the liver (what we in English refer to "as the pit of the stomach").

---

[10]An illustration of the difference between Greek and Hebrew thought may be seen in the way in which the NT quotes Deuteronomy 6:4. The Hebrew says, "You shall love the Lord your God with all your heart, with all your soul, and with all your strength." But the NT Greek quotation says, ". . . with all your heart, soul, *mind* and strength" (Mark 12:30). The reason for the difference is that "heart" in Hebrew includes the functions of thought and decision-making, while "heart" in Greek does not include those functions. Thus the Greek word for "mind" must be added to the quotation in order to capture the full intent of the Hebrew statement.

Thus, a person's "heart" is the control-center of the personality. Here we see what a person really is in himself or herself.

So what does it mean when it is said that a person does something with a "whole (or "complete") heart" (*leb shalem*)? Surely it means that they are undivided in their thinking, their will, and their choices. Much the same thing was said using *tamim* in Ps. 119:80 "May my heart be *whole* regarding your statutes, in order that I may not be disgraced"(author's translation).[11] Is that possible? Is it possible for one of us humans, deeply perverse as we are, to give really exclusive commitment to something outside of ourselves, as the covenant calls for?[12] Is it possible for us to have an undivided heart? According to the Old Testament such a thing is possible, and I want to look in some detail at the examples which are given there because they have direct bearing upon the question we are addressing in this chapter.

The first occurrence of this concept (chronologically) is in 1 Chronicles 12:38 where we are told that all the men of war came to Hebron with "a perfect heart" to make David king of Israel. That is, the author is telling us that there was neither uncertainty nor division among the warriors over who should be the king. These people were "single-minded" in their devotion to David and their determination to make him king.

All the rest of the occurrences of this phrase relate to single-minded devotion to God. It is David who prays that Solomon should have a "perfect heart" toward God (1 Chron. 28:9; 29:19). Both of these references are very important to the point being made here. The first says: "You, my son Solomon, know the God of your father and serve him with a *perfect* heart and with a willing spirit, because the LORD inquires into every heart and understands every means of forming (*yetser*) thoughts" (Author's translation).

---

[11] See also Pss. 101:2 and 119:80 where forms of *tmm* are used with "heart," showing the connection between the two concepts.

[12] Note Prov. 28:18 which directly contrasts a perfect (*tamim*) walk with perverse (*ne`qas*) ways. So also the perfect (*tom*) heart of Ps. 101:2 is contrasted with the perverse (*rahab*) heart of v. 5.

The second says: "To Solomon, my son, give a *perfect* heart in order to carefully keep your commandments, your testimonies, and your statutes, and to do them all, and in order to build this great building for which I have provided" (Author's translation).

These two passages are each important for what they establish about the heart that is whole, or perfect, toward God. The first one is significant because it establishes that the perfect heart is so in relation to the fundamental human problem discussed in the previous chapter: the corrupted power of imagination. Solomon is called upon by David to do two things: to have a living experience with his father's God, and to serve him with an absolute loyalty which is an expression of the glad desire of Solomon's whole person. Why is he to do this? Because God is concerned about our "hearts" and he understands perfectly well the perverted character of our thought processes. So David is telling Solomon what he himself has learned about living for God. God does not want anything less than all we are, because that alone will be sufficient to come to grips with the terrible perverseness that has come to hold humanity in its grip.

But what is the character of this wholeheartedness? We need to be very careful here because of the primarily sentimental connotations of "heart" in modern English. It is very easy to conclude that what is being talked about here is great enthusiasm for God, or great excitement about our spiritual growth, or something of that sort. The second of these two passages makes it quite clear this is not what David is talking about at all. To have a perfect heart toward God is to obey his covenant stipulations. It is to make him the absolute Lord of our lives, to submit to his will, to call sin what he calls sin, to call righteousness what he calls righteousness, and to view people as he views people. Being wholeheartedly God's has much less to do with how we feel about God than it does with letting him slash out of our lives everything which stands as a rival to him so that he can fill our lives with himself and transform the very way we image reality.

In 1 Chronicles 29:9 we see the kind of chain reaction which this kind of response to God produces. Because David's devotion to God was pure and complete, and because that was his chief desire for his son, the leadership of the nation was motivated to respond to God in the same way with their gifts for the Temple. This building was not intended to be a testimony to the greatness of the Davidic dynasty, but to the greatness of God, and the leaders had no difficulty in joining in the project without reservation. The result of the leaders' response is joy on the part of the people. Why should this be so? Why should the people care how their leaders reacted? They care because leaders who are completely surrendered to God are much less likely to oppress their people in an attempt to aggrandize themselves. It is not hard to submit to the leadership of one who has submitted himself to God.

Solomon had caught the flavor of his father's life, as he makes plain in his charge to the people at the dedication of the Temple (1 Kings 8:56-61). He tells them that his goal for the Temple is that it will be the means of all the peoples of earth coming to know that Yahweh is God and there is no other (v. 60). But, he goes on to say, if that goal is to be reached then the people of Israel will have to have perfect hearts toward God so as to live out his statutes, and carefully keep all his commandments (v. 61). These statements have several important ramifications. They show us that the worldwide vision was not something that originated with the Church. And the logic of this vision should be quite clear: if there is only one God, and he is the sole creator of the earth, then all peoples should know and recognize him. And if a person recognizes and knows this God in any true sense, worship cannot help but follow. So Solomon envisions all the peoples of earth coming to this place to worship the One God who has chosen to put his name here. But it will not be the splendor of some earthly building that draws people to God. Rather it will be the glory of his own person as it is depicted in the lives of his worshippers. So Solomon recognizes that unless the people of God are completely submitted to God in unreserved obedience, manifesting the life of God in their daily walk, the Temple will accomplish nothing. The Temple will be a symbol of the beauty of the Divine/human relationship. And if that relationship does not truly exist as a result of perfect hearts, then the beauty of the Temple will be no more than that of a prostitute.

Isaiah captures this connection between symbol and reality to startling effect in his first two chapters. In chapter 1, he speaks of God's disgust at the temple worship, having God say, "The multitude of your sacrifices— what are they to me? ...I have no pleasure in the blood of bulls and lambs and goats" (1:11). Why is this worship displeasing to him? Because it is not an expression of hearts which are fully surrendered to God as demonstrated in obedience in ethical righteousness. What God wants is made clear in vv. 16-17:

> "Wash and make yourselves clean.
> Take your evil deeds out of my sight!
> Stop doing wrong,
>   learn to do right!
> Seek justice,
>   encourage the oppressed.
> Defend the cause of the fatherless,
>   plead the case of the widow."

But what happens when people with perfect hearts do obey God and live in ways which reveal his holy character to the world? Isaiah shows this in the first four verses of his second chapter (which are duplicated in Micah 4:1-4). Just as unholy living brings the Temple worship into disgrace, holy living will bring worldwide honor to the Temple. The peoples of the earth will say,

> "Come, let us go up to the mountain of the LORD
>   to the house of the God of Jacob.
> He will teach us his ways
>   so that we may walk in his paths.
> The law will go out from Zion,
>   the word of the LORD from Jerusalem. (2:3)

So what instruction should the people of Israel draw from this prophecy? Isaiah gives it in v. 5: "Come, O house of Jacob, let us walk in the light of the LORD." The symbol and the reality are forever intertwined. The Temple will be the center for the teaching of the glorious truths about God. But unless those truths are enshrined in the lives of people who are wholly submitted to God, the Temple worship will bring nothing but disgust from God and reproach from the world.

All this is painfully true in the life of Solomon. There is a bitter irony in David's prayer for Solomon and in Solomon's stirring words to his people. For we the readers know that this is exactly what is going to fail to come to pass in Solomon's life. Having known so much and understood so well, he yet in the end makes a shipwreck of his life, and more tragically, of the life of his nation. 1 Kings 11:4 reports the event in terse words: "When Solomon was old, his wives led his heart astray after other gods, and his heart was not *perfect* towards his God, like the heart of his father David" (Author's translation). What David in spite of his failures had known, Solomon in spite of his successes lost. It is possible to belong to God exclusively and to live out his life, but Solomon allowed that exclusive devotion to God, in which every decision is taken with concern for God's way and God's honor, to be diluted and thus lost. Undoubtedly his marriages were political in nature, designed to cement alliances with surrounding countries. Thus, he could claim that they were necessary in order to achieve the kind of world leadership that God had promised to the Davidic dynasty. But if it was necessary, then it was also necessary that these wives be brought into the great Temple Solomon was building, there to declare their allegiance to Solomon's God.

Whenever the world's methods are used for God's work, we must be doubly careful that those methods are sanctified by the fire of God. Perhaps Solomon thought his relationship with God was so secure that nothing could touch it. To his sorrow, he learned this is never the case. Our will, our decisions, our affections are never static. A heart that is perfect toward God does indeed have a new set of inclinations, inclinations to obey rather than to disobey, but unless those inclinations are carefully nourished from day to day, they will wither and die, like Solomon's did.

The effects of Solomon's sins carried out through the rest of Israel's history, but especially through the next two generations. By his own lack of wisdom Solomon's son Rehoboam exacerbated the problems Solomon's faulty policies had begun, and David's and Solomon's kingdom broke in two. Interestingly, Chronicles presents Rehoboam in a relatively better light than Kings does, but it is nowhere indicated that Rehoboam was a man wholly given over to the obedience of God. In the case of Rehoboam's son Abijah, the situation is stated explicitly. 1 Kings 15:3 tells us that "He committed all the sins his father had done before him; his heart was not *perfect* toward the LORD his God as was the heart of David his ancestor" (author's translation).

But fortunately the fragrance of a life lived entirely to God can blow across the generations. As we noted earlier, while God restricts the effects of sin to two or three generations, he spreads the effect of righteousness to a thousand generations. So we find in David's great grandson Asa, a man whose heart was as *perfect* toward God as was that of David his ancestor (1 Kings 15:14). It would be interesting to know exactly what the line of influence was which brought Asa back to this happy condition. Clearly it was not through the influence of his grandmother, Maacah, because she was an idolator (1 Kings 15:13). Rather, the line of faithfulness extended through a series of people who are unknown to the world—people who, on the face of it, were insignificant and unimportant. But in fact, as they continued to give their hearts to God unreservedly, as they continued to live wholly for God, they carried the priceless seed that would spring up in an Asa whose faithfulness would pull the nation back from the brink of disaster once more.

The description of Asa in 1 Kings 15:14 (and paralleled in 1 Chron. 15:17) is significant in that it underlines a point made earlier. That point was that to be complete, or perfect, in one's devotion to God and in one's obedience to him does not necessarily imply perfect performance. That is the point that the Scripture makes with regard to Asa. The text says, "Although he did not remove the high places, Asa's heart was *perfect* toward the LORD all his life." As nearly as we can determine, the worship of Yahweh had become increasingly decentralized after the Ark's capture by the Philistines and its 20-year sojourn in Kiriath-Jearim (1 Sam. 7:1). Prior to that, the presence of the Ark and the Tabernacle at Shiloh, where they had apparently been from the time of the Conquest, had acted as a restraint upon the fragmentation of worship which would have normally accompanied the fragmentation of the nation during the Judges period.[13] But with the loss of that center, it seems that Yahwistic worship centers began to spring up in many places. There may have even been rival tabernacles. Notice that the discussion of events at Nob in 1 Samuel 21 seems to presuppose the presence of the Tabernacle there, as does the description of Gibeon in 1 Kings 3. At the same time, 1 Kings 1 and 2 clearly imply that the Tabernacle was in Jerusalem. While it is possible this is the same Tabernacle being moved from place to place, the other possibility must be entertained as well.

The reason this fragmentation of worship had been forbidden in Deuteronomy was because it would almost necessarily lead to a fragmentation of the person of God. That is, each locality where Yahweh would be worshipped would come to think of him as a different deity than the one who was worshipped over the hill a few miles away. With this development polytheism would not be far away, and with that transcendence would be lost. Nevertheless, it is apparent that the disasters of the Judges period led to a general loss of attention to the written Torah, so that in succeeding years even good people like Samuel and the early Solomon had no conscience about such worship. This was probably even more true by the time of Asa. Thus, although Asa was clearly disobeying an express command of God, and was thus exhibiting a performance that fell a good ways short of perfect, he was doing so in ignorance. According to the text his devotion to God was perfect; that is, he was completely surrendered to God and was determined to obey him to the full extent of his awareness. We may assume that if the book of Deuteronomy had been brought to his attention as it was to Josiah's, Asa would have been just as assiduous in obeying it as Josiah was.[14]

Another example of this principle that the perfect heart is not

---

[13]For an example of that fragmentation occurring anyway, see Judges 17-18.

[14]It is interesting that Chronicles (2 Chron. 16) does not give so positive a report of Asa. To that writer, Asa's treaty with the Syrians betrayed a lack of trust that shed a bad light upon the level of Asa's trust in God. One wonders if this interpretation was in some ways prompted by the need for the returnees from the exile to maintain their separation from their pagan neighbors.

inseparably linked to perfect performance may be seen in a reverse example in the life of King Amaziah. 2 Chronicles 25:2 reports that Amaziah "did what was right in the sight of the LORD." The word translated "right" is *yasar*, which is used to parallel forms of *tmm* several times when that root is being used to talk of perfect devotion to God (1 Kings 9:5; Job 1:1, 8, 2:3; Ps. 37:37). It speaks of behavior that is all it might be expected to be in God's sight. In short, it is a very high commendation of Amaziah and the quality of his life. But then comes the terse, but devastating comment, "but not with a *perfect heart*." That is, Amaziah was a man whose moral behavior was outstanding. He was concerned to keep the law as he knew it (25:4) and he was obedient to the prophets God gave him (vv. 7-9). But he was not obedient out of a total surrender of his will, his decision-making capacities and his affections to God. The text does not specify what his motivations for an upright life were, but on the basis of experience we may suggest that one possibility was pride. He wished to be known as a good man. Another possibility is expedience. Under all the circumstances, this behavior was likely to achieve the best results. But one more possibility must be considered. Perhaps Amaziah genuinely did believe in God and genuinely did want to serve him, but simply at some crisis point in his life where God asked for all of his life without reserve, Amaziah was unable to give that much of himself.

So we have this interesting juxtaposition; an Asa whose commitment to God was absolute even though his obedience fell short of all that it might have been, and an Amaziah whose performance was as upright as anyone could expect, *even God*, but who never finally yielded the control center of himself to God. What does such a juxtaposition say about God's will and the possibilities for human life? Surely it says that what God wants above all—and what it is possible for us humans to give—is a life which is totally given over to him. This is the heart of the covenant. This is a life that exists for one purpose: the service and the glory of God. An inescapable component of such a perfect heart is obedience. It could not be otherwise. But God does not want obedience. He wants obedience which is the natural outflow of a heart totally given over to him. If that obedience is not all that it might be in other circumstances, or in other persons, he is willing to work with that fact. What he does not want is obedience which is offered in place of the perfect heart. Such obedience then become a means of attempted self-justification, a fruitless enterprise.

While we are not told that Jehoshaphat's heart was perfect, 2 Chronicles 17:6 says that his heart was "high" ("lifted up" AV, "devoted" NIV, "courageous" NRSV) in the ways of the LORD," while 1 Kings 22:43 tells us that he did not depart from his father Asa's ways, and did what was right (*yasar*) in the eyes of the Lord. But perhaps a more telling reflection of his character is found in his admonition to the Levites, priests, and leaders whom he appointed to administer the religious affairs of Jerusalem. He told them, "You must do this in the fear of the Lord, in true faithfulness, and with a *perfect* heart" (2 Chron. 19:9). This is perhaps as full a description of "true religion" in the Old Testament as it is possible to find. One's behavior grows out of a correct understanding of who we are and who God is, out of a determination that we should be true in all our relationships as he is true, and out of a life center which is wholly given over to God. If this was not a description of Jehoshaphat's own life, it certainly shows an understanding of the issues and a belief that such a life was a possibility. It also helps us to remember that we are not talking about a word here, but about a concept.

The next occurrence (and the final one) of the phrase "perfect heart" is found exactly where we would expect it: in the narrative of the life and ministry of King Hezekiah. From Jehoshaphat to Hezekiah was a long, dry spell in the annals of Judean kingship. There were some kings who were generally obedient, like Amaziah, Uzziah, and Jotham, and while the religious situation did not get markedly worse during their reigns, neither did it get markedly better. Under Jotham's successor Ahaz, the situation did get worse, so that Hezekiah came to the throne at a moment of crisis. Would Judah follow its sister Israel into the oblivion of Assyrian exile because of a persistent denial of God's exclusive lordship? Or would a leader who belonged unreservedly to God bring Judah to a moment of reprieve? Of course we know that the latter was the case. Hezekiah not only replicated the works of his more faithful ancestors, he went beyond them. Unlike Asa and Jehoshaphat, he destroyed the high places and brought about the kind of centralization of worship which had been envisioned in the Torah. Second Chronicles also tells about the refurbishing of the Temple and the reorganization of the priests. Thus it comes as no surprise when we hear Hezekiah, in a moment of personal crisis, having been told his death is imminent, cry out, "Remember, O LORD, how I have walked before you in true faithfulness and with a *perfect* heart, and have done what is good in your eyes" (2 Kings 20:3). He had indeed lived a life of manifest obedience flowing out of a life center that was wholly given over to God. And God seems to confirm the truth of that claim in his response of giving Hezekiah a reprieve for another 15 years.

If there were one more person in whose account we would expect to find some reference to a "perfect heart," it would surely be King Josiah, the last of Judah's "good" kings. In fact, he is considered by both Kings and Chronicles to be the one king who "did it all right." He was the one who expunged paganism the most thoroughly from the country. And in fact the description that we have of him, if it lacks the specific phrase "perfect heart," surely shows that he fulfilled the spirit of that idea in a dramatic way. In 2 Kings 23:25 we read this: "Neither before nor after Josiah was there a king like him who turned to the LORD as he did—with all his heart and with all his soul and with all his strength, in accordance with all the Law of Moses."

What I have been trying to show in this chapter is that despite the general, and repeated, failure of the nation as a whole to live up to the expectations of their covenant with God, this was not because of the impossibility of a human's doing so. It is true that we are deeply depraved, and have been so since conception, if we accept that Psalm 51's statement is not merely a figure of speech. It is also true that a mere superficial decision to live for God, such as the one made by the people of Israel at the foot of Sinai, will never be sufficient to bring us to that place where a wholly-surrendered heart issues in a life of true faithfulness and genuine obedience. Nevertheless, such a life is still possible and it is still expected by God. It is possible to be perfect—whole, complete, undivided—in our devotion to him, and if our obedience is always unintentionally limited by matters beyond our control, such as ignorance or imperception, it is nevertheless possible for a person to give an obedience which is perfect, that is, flawless, utterly without blame. However, that kind of a heart and that kind of a life are never merely the result of human effort, and that will be the subject of the next chapter.

5

The Gift of the Holy Spirit
in the Old Testament

What is the problem with humanity from the Old Testament's perspective? Several different images are used, as we have already seen. There is the wicked, or perverse, heart. There is the evil imagination. But there is another image that is perhaps even more helpful than these when we think of an inclination to evil. This is the twisted spirit. The Hebrew word which is translated "spirit" has many of the same connotations as the English word "spirit." That is, it can be used to speak of the general trend of a group of people, or of a locality, just as we might speak of "the spirit of the meeting." Slightly more specifically we might speak of the team's having "a lot of spirit," meaning that there is a particular energy or dynamism about what they do. Or we might speak of "the human spirit," meaning that indefinable something which makes a human alive and is gone when a person dies. To these, Hebrew adds two more concrete usages that are quite logical. The Hebrew word may mean "breath," that invisible something which goes out one last time when a person dies, and it can mean "wind," that invisible power which moves solid, tangible things. When we are aware that the word has all these connotations we realize that when Jesus, in talking with Nicodemus, moved easily from talking about wind to talking about the Spirit, it was because his native language (Aramaic, a sister language of Hebrew) had already made the connections for him (John 3:5-8).[15]

It is the prophet Hosea who is especially helpful to us in understanding the Old Testament use of "spirit" in relation to the human condition. He says that we humans are afflicted with a "spirit of prostitution."

> "They consult a wooden idol
>   and are answered by a stick of wood.
> A spirit of prostitution leads them astray;
>   they are unfaithful to their God." (4:12)
> "Their deeds do not permit them
>   to return to their God
> A spirit of prostitution is in their heart;
>   they do not acknowledge [know] the Lord." (5:4)

What does he mean by such statements? And how do they relate to our problem as humans? Almost certainly he means that there is something wrong with that which motivates us, that which provides the driving force in our lives. There is a certain tendency about us, a certain attitude, a certain way of responding. And what is that tendency? It is a tendency to promiscuousness, a tendency to inconstancy, a tendency to faithlessness. The kind of response God wants from us, a complete and irrevocable surrender of the control-center of our lives, is the very kind of a response we are least likely to give to him, says Hosea.

All of this goes straight back to the Garden of Eden. What was the sin of Adam and Eve? They succumbed to the temptation to determine right and wrong for themselves. The result is of course tragedy, the ongoing tragedy of which we are still a part. It is as though a compass decides that it will determine for itself where the magnetic pole is. This is a denial of the compass' true nature, and it is also to make the compass useless for its true purpose. Like the prostitute, we have decided that we will determine for ourselves where our true pleasure

---

[15]The Greek word "pneuma" makes the same connections between "wind" and "spirit."

lies. Above all, we are determined not to find it in an exclusive relation to our true husband. The result is that our gifts are squandered on those who do not care for us, who only wish to use us.

Thus Hosea is saying that there is something wrong with the whole human outlook, with the whole human approach to life. The same sense is found in Psalm 78:8 which says, "They [the next generation] would not be like their forefathers—a stubborn and rebellious generation, whose hearts were not fixed on God, whose spirits were not truly faithful to him" (Author's translation).

Zechariah speaks of a "spirit of impurity" which needs to be removed from the land (13:2).

Thus the Hebrew people realized that their problem was one of the spirit. If they were ever as a people to fulfill God's expectations for them, if they were ever to fulfill the spirit of the covenant and serve God with perfect hearts in flawless obedience, then something was going to have to be done about the human spirit. This is nowhere more clearly revealed than in Psalm 51. As a result of the terrible things he has done, David recognizes a depth of depravity in himself that he had not even imagined before: "Surely I was sinful at birth, sinful from the time my mother conceived me" (v. 5).

Because of this, he asks God to do a radical work in him. he asks that God will make him true in the very depth of his personality, that is, that he will give David genuine moral discernment on the deepest level: "Surely you desire truth in the inner parts; you teach me wisdom in the inmost place" (v. 6).

But David goes further. He asks for a "pure (or clean) heart," (v. 10) and the structure of the rest of the sentence helps us to understand what such a phrase means. Such a heart would be the result of a different spirit than had prevailed in David previously (v.10). Instead of that inconstant spirit of prostitution which divides itself between one lover and another with its unclean heart, David recognizes the need for a different kind of spirit, another kind of dynamic, in his life. He speaks of it as a "steadfast" spirit. The sense of the Hebrew word is of being solidly fixed or established. David realizes that the only hope of having a genuinely pure heart, one which belongs to God through and through, is if something fairly radical is done to his human spirit. Having one's heart wholly devoted to God was not merely a matter of wishing it to be so. God must change our spirits. Was it this recognition which made David plead so earnestly for a perfect heart for his son? In any case, it is surely not accidental that it was having too many wives that in the end kept Solomon from having a perfect[16] heart toward God. A pure heart is impossible unless God had done something to correct our inconstant spirit.

Not only does David long for a spirit which has one fixed pole in God, he also asks God for a spirit which is free to give itself away (v. 12). Interestingly, he sees such a spirit as the key to joy in one's life. The person whose only reference point is himself or herself may experience exhilaration or excitement, but that deep abiding delight in living, even when the living is dark and difficult, will forever escape them. David has learned this to his own dismay. He knows that joy is a byproduct of a relationship with God in which he is constantly delivered from himself ("the joy of your salvation"), and he realizes that he has lost this joy because of a spirit which is fixated upon what it can get, not what it can give. English translators have had difficulty finding a single word to translate the idea. AV has "free spirit," while NKJV has "generous spirit." NIV and NRSV have "willing spirit," and JB has "spirit steady and willing." The idea behind the word is that of large-hearted generosity. Perhaps on the surface this concept might seem at odds with the previous one. How can an established spirit be one which freely gives itself away? But that is just the point. No prostitute ever gives her true self away to her lovers. She cannot, or she will surely lose herself in a bottomless pit. No, she may give her body, but herself, her spirit, she must jealously guard for herself. So it is with the prostituted human spirit. Having embraced a hundred illicit lovers, we are no longer free to give ourselves away, even if someone were to come along to whom we wanted to give ourselves. We must protect ourselves for ourselves, for no one else will.

---

[16]Remember that at its root "pure" means to be all one thing, and not adulterated with any other thing. Thus a "whole" or "perfect" heart is identical to a "pure" heart.

But suppose something were to happen to give us a spirit which was truly fixed on one point, in one relationship, what then? What if we knew in our deepest hearts that this Lover was not out merely to use us and throw us away, but wished to give himself irrevocably to us? Could we not then abandon all our fears and lavish all the gifts we have upon him? Not only that, but we could give our gifts away to others, secure in the abundant love of God. This is the kind of picture painted in Isaiah 32:1-8, where the prophet describes the Messianic kingdom as one in which righteous government and security will prevail. In his description Isaiah draws a sharp contrast between wickedness, or foolishness, and nobility, or generosity. A noble spirit is a large-hearted, generous one, and it is in sharp contrast to that typical human spirit which foolishly acts and thinks as though its interests are the only ones in the world.

> "No longer will the fool be called *noble*
>   nor the scoundrel be highly respected.
> For the fool speaks folly,
>   his mind is busy with evil:
> He practices ungodliness
>   and spreads error concerning the LORD;
> the hungry he leaves empty
>   and from the thirsty he withholds water.
> The scoundrel's methods are wicked,
>   he makes up evil schemes
> to destroy the poor with lies,
>   even when the plea of the needy is just.
> But the noble man makes noble plans,
>   and by noble deeds he stands." (Isaiah 32:5-8)

This is the kind of spirit that David has come to recognize he needs. Humanly speaking, the picture we have of David in the Bible shows a remarkably generous man. But David recognizes that he cannot merely rest upon whatever level of behavior his inherited temperament may normally produce. He needs a spirit that is free to give itself away because it has been supernaturally fixed upon God.

The connection between this kind of spirit and joy is illustrated in 1 Chronicles 29:9. There we read that the people had been moved to great joy because their leaders had generously volunteered themselves and their possessions to God out of perfect hearts. Why should this behavior have made the people happy? Perhaps one reason is that leaders who are wholly dedicated to God as shown by their generosity can be expected to manifest that same kind of behavior towards their people. But another reason is simply the infectiousness of joy. The joy of the leaders in their freedom in giving was catching. It still is.

But between these two requests for a change in spirit is the one that is the key to the other two. Between the request for an established spirit and a willing, or free, spirit is the plea that God should not take his *holy* spirit from David. In other words, the key to the new spirit that David is asking for is the presence of God's Spirit. It seems probable that this request grows out of the memory of Saul, a memory that must have gained horrifying power at this time in David's life. For once Saul had been dramatically filled with God's Spirit, as David had been after him. But then through disobedience and rebellion, Saul had lost that intimate presence, and the vacuum had been filled with an altogether different spirit. That horrifying possibility must have gripped David with an icy hand during this experience. So David begs that God would not take his Spirit from him. If he is ever to know the kind of alteration of spirit that he is praying for, it can only come through the Spirit of God at work within him.

Here in a nutshell is the Old Testament understanding of the issue that we are discussing: (1) There is a flaw in the human spirit which manifests itself in the prostitution of our best gifts and abilities. Instead of using them for our Creator and his glory, we try to use them for ourselves with the result that our very ways of thinking have become corrupted; (2) The human spirit must be renewed in some way from without. Any attempt to turn over a new leaf, as it were, finds the stain spreading upward from the previous pages. No clearer example of this can be found than in the story of Noah and his sons after the flood; (3) The renewal of the human spirit can only occur in connection with the Holy Spirit, the divine Spirit, taking up residence in us.

This recognition of the necessity of the Spirit's enabling us to do what the human spirit could not has a long history of development in the Old Testament text. In general there is a movement from the level of superhuman ability in various fields to an awareness of the implications of these phenomena for the moral character of humans. What we see in the various accounts is a recognition that the person in question is performing at a level which is far beyond that which the unaided human spirit could be expected to do. So the Pharaoh recognizes in Joseph a wisdom which is more than human, and he asks where he could find a more likely candidate for administrator than in the man "in whom is the spirit of God" (Gen. 41:38). At this point it is not necessary to suppose Pharaoh was a believer in the biblical God to have made this observation. He is simply recognizing that there is a supernatural spirit at work in this young man, one that far surpasses anything normally expected of the human spirit.[17]

In the same way, when it came time to construct the Tabernacle, with all of the intricate craftsmanship which that wonderful complex required, who among these former slaves could have been expected to possess such talents? Yet a man named Bezaleel came forward with his assistant and supervised the entire project. How was he able to do such a thing? Native ability? No, the Bible tells us that he was gifted with all these special skills as a result of having been filled with the Holy Spirit (Exod. 31:2-5; 35:30-33). Furthermore, we are told that God gave him the ability to teach others the necessary skills of craftsmanship (Exod. 35:34). What the text is saying is that Bezaleel possessed gifts which were more than human ability could explain. There was another power, another ability, at work in him, one which could only be understood as having come from God.

The next reference of this sort is found in the narrative of Moses. Numbers 11 tells about a crisis in the leadership of the people of God. Moses is worn out with the daily stresses of trying to lead an unruly people. So God tells him to take the elders to the Tabernacle where he will "take of the Spirit that is on you and put the Spirit on them" (v. 17). That is, Moses was possessed of a supernatural leadership ability; what he was doing was something which the

---

[17]Many years later the Babylonian royalty were to say the same thing about Daniel (4:9; 5:11, 14).

unaided human spirit could not do. Now God is proposing to extend that superhuman ability to those who served under Moses. Although there is no specific description of Joshua's being filled with the Spirit, Numbers 27:18 speaks of him as a man in whom the Spirit is, and Deuteronomy 34:9 says that he had a "spirit of wisdom" because of Moses' having laid hands on him. Perhaps we are to conclude that his initial experience of such a filling occurred during this event described in Numbers 11. At any rate, Joshua also is being described as one whose leadership abilities were not merely human. There was a spirit about him which spoke of the presence of God at work in what he said and did.

In Numbers 24:2 we encounter another example in which being filled with the Spirit expresses behavior which is contrary to that normally expected of the human spirit. The professional prophet Baalam has been called by the King of Moab to put a curse upon the people of Israel. That is, he is expected to use the remarkable skills that he has acquired through a lifetime of study and application to manipulate divine power on behalf of a client. But even at the outset Baalam expresses some doubt about whether he can do that in this case. He is here dealing with God, not a god, and Baalam confesses that he cannot manipulate him (22:8). In the end, Baalam speaks the exact opposite of the word he had been hired to speak: not a word of curse, but a word of blessing. What happened? The Bible explains it very succinctly: "the Spirit of God came upon him" (Num. 24:2). He did not say what normal human ability and insight would have prompted him to say. Rather, he said something quite unexpected and out of the ordinary.

In the same way, the "judge"[18] Gideon, looked at from a merely human perspective, was a coward and a man of small propensity to

---

[18]"Judge" has been placed in quotation marks here because the Hebrew word being translated does not really connote what "judge" does in English. These figures in Israel's history did not have to do primarily with the administration of law as judges do in modern civilization. In Hebrew the word used (*shophet*) describes someone who brings order out of chaos. Because this may include handing down decisions about disputes between persons, "judge" has come to be used in the English translations, but "champion" would describe them equally well.

faith. When we first meet him he is trying to thresh grain in a wine vat, the most ineffective place for that purpose (Judg. 6:11). Threshing floors were out in the open where the wind could separate the chaff from the grain. Wine vats tended to be low in the valleys where both those making the wine and the wine itself could be sheltered. But the open threshing floor ran a serious risk of attracting the unwanted attention of the enemy, so Gideon was trying to protect himself in a sheltered place even though it was not very well suited to the task at hand. In the same way, when God commanded him to destroy his father's Baal altar, he obeyed, but at night because of his fear (Judg. 6:27). Furthermore, when God informed Gideon that he had been chosen for special service, his response was not like that of the virgin Mary many years later, who humbly believed the impossible. Rather, Gideon required not one, but two supernatural proofs. None of this is to denigrate Gideon; he had good reasons for his fear, and the kinds of things the angel said to him really were unbelievable. But how shall we explain his later behavior when he manifests great courage and remarkable faith? The biblical answer is just what we would expect: Gideon was filled with the Holy Spirit (Judg. 6:34). Gideon's own spirit was not capable of the things he did, but there was another Spirit at work in him. Similar things are said of the judges Othniel (Judg. 3:10) and Jephthah (11:29), and especially of Samson (13:25; 14:16, 19; 15:14, 19). With Samson it is primarily the superhuman feats of strength which are explained by reference to the Spirit of God filling him. Again the point is that these were activities of which the normal human spirit would be incapable.

The theme of Spirit-filled leadership continues into the monarchy with Saul and David. In the case of Saul, the references are very explicit. Samuel, when he is describing in advance what will happen to Saul as evidence of God having chosen him as king, makes it very clear that the Spirit's fullness will be the key by which Saul will rule (1 Sam. 10:6-7). There are two particular features of what happened to Saul which are very important for our consideration here. The first is prophesying, and the second is "a new heart." Above we noticed that Baalam was empowered to speak the word of God through the

Holy Spirit. Here, the same thing occurs again. While it would be false to say that we understand everything about the phenomena that accompany prophecy in the Old Testament,[19] there is certainly the unmistakable element of receiving and declaring a communication from God. The Spirit of the Lord is the one who communicates God's will to us and through us. To experience the presence of God in a real and intimate way is inseparable from a realization of his will and purpose. God is above all a God of communication; he wants his people to know him. And this is the Spirit's task.

A second important feature of the phenomena surrounding Saul's spirit-filling is his receiving of "a new heart." This is the first time in narrative in which the concepts which we saw earlier in Psalm 51 are expressed. Here we have a clear connection between Spirit-filling and moral renovation. We also have the connection between the "heart" and the Spirit. It is the Spirit who gives us the ability to live wholly for God, an ability that we lack otherwise. Our hearts are terribly divided, and the imagination by which our thoughts ("the thoughts of our hearts") are shaped is deeply and utterly corrupted. God expects us to share his character; that is his goal for us. Yet, as the Hebrew people learned to their dismay, there is that in us which seems to prevent us from reaching that goal, sincere though our efforts may be. What is to be done? Here it is: the Spirit of God must fill us, communicating the character and will of God to us, and giving us a heart which belongs wholly to God.

The great tragedy of all of this, of course, is that this wonderful potential was never realized in Saul. Whatever experiences with God we may have had, he never removes our capacity for free will, and unless we continue to cooperate with the Spirit who is filling us, there is always the possibility of regression. That is what happened with Saul, beginning in an inability to wait for God (1 Sam. 13) and

---

[19]It is not clear whether some form of ecstatic behavior was involved in Saul's experience of spirit-filling. Later on, it clearly was (1 Sam. 19:23-24), but that was after the mania which would eventually destroy Saul had gotten its hold upon him, so it is doubtful whether that experience should be used to explain the first. To assume that "prophesy" necessarily involves frenzy (cf. NRSV in both 1 Sam. 10 and 19) seems unwarranted to me.

culminating in a refusal to obey Him (1 Sam. 15). When we analyze the entire Saul narrative, we see a man who, despite his height and good looks, never really felt worth very much. On his inauguration day he was so embarrassed by the attention that he hid among the baggage. So he was never able to allow the Spirit to make him self-forgetful. He was always afraid that someone would discover how little the real Saul was who lived in the large, impressive frame (cf. 1 Sam. 15:17, "Though you are little in your own eyes, are you not the head of the tribes of Israel?" [NRSV]). In the end this fearfulness assumed the proportions of paranoia, and there was no room left for the Holy Spirit in Saul's life. With that tragic picture stamped on David's mind, we can understand the terror underlying David's pleas that the Spirit not leave him.

What lessons about Spirit-filling should we draw from the life of Saul? I suggest that there are three that are most important. First, when the Spirit fills us, he wants to communicate the character and will of God to us and through us, and he wants to remake the control-center of our lives, so that it is dominated without contest by him. But second, the full realization of the work of the Spirit is neither automatic nor instant. For him to do all that he wants is a matter of a lifetime—a lifetime of patient and faithful cooperation with him. Third, to have been once really and genuinely filled with the Spirit is no guarantee that we will finish the course successfully. Refusal to allow him to do all the work he wishes to do in us is to put ourselves in grave jeopardy.

David is the last of Israel's rulers of whom it is said that they were filled with the Holy Spirit (1 Sam. 16:13). Perhaps we should not make too much of that in that others are said to have had a perfect heart, as we have seen above. However, at the least we need to draw the correlation between this description of David and the one that has come to characterize him so widely. Who was David? He was a man after God's own heart (1 Sam. 13:14; Acts 13:22). What does a phrase like that mean? Surely among other things it describes a man whose concerns are the same as God's. He is not concerned about his own image, or his own success, he is concerned for God. That is evident in the first story about him in the Bible. When he realized that the giant Goliath was blaspheming the name of God, he had only one concern: putting a stop to that right then! That passion for God and for God's name and for God's honor was the underlying foundation of all that David did, and this helps us to understand the very different fates of Saul and David. From one perspective David's sins may be considered as being much worse than Saul's. After all, he committed adultery and judicial murder, while Saul offered a sacrifice, made a foolish vow, and didn't wholly wipe out an enemy people. But David's sins were a momentary slip in contrast to the settled focus of his life, while Saul's were but one expression of the self-obsession which had come to rule his thinking. So again we see, as in Psalm 51, the direct connection between the heart and its condition, and the life of the Spirit. If we are to fulfill God's goals for us, it will only be possible through the fullness of the Spirit of God counterbalancing and overruling the spirit of prostitution that characterizes human behavior otherwise.

This truth becomes even clearer in the prophets when they speak of the Holy Spirit and his work. In Isaiah 32 the prophet is describing the moral situation in Judah. The people, following their leaders, have forsaken their trust in God and have turned to the nations around them for their hope. What will be the result of such a foolish course of action? Isaiah declares it in no uncertain terms:

> "The fortress will be abandoned,
>   the noisy city deserted;
> citadel and watchtower will become a wasteland forever,
>   the delight of donkeys, a pasture for flocks, (32:14)

This was what he had predicted with steady consistency throughout his book thus far. If you trust anything else in place of God it will eventually turn on you and destroy you. What was Israel's problem? They had forsaken God and gone after other lovers, and in so doing, the justice and righteousness that God had intended would characterize their community had been lost. In short, they had broken their covenant with God.

So what will God do? Will he wipe them out, as he has a perfect right to do on the basis of their own oath? No he will not. When the destruction which they have brought upon themselves for not trusting God has worked its full effect, then God will appear and do what? Notice that the sentence just quoted is incomplete, and this is the way it continues:

> "till the Spirit is poured upon us from on high,
>> and the desert becomes a fertile field,
>> and the fertile field seems like a forest
> Justice will dwell in the desert
>> and righteousness live in the fruitful field.
> The fruit of righteousness will be peace;
>> the effect of righteousness will be quietness and
>>> confidence forever.
> My people will live in peaceful dwelling places,
>> in secure homes,
>> in undisturbed places of rest.
> Though hail flattens the forest
>> and the city is leveled completely,
> how blessed you will be,
>> sowing your seed by every stream,
>> and letting your oxen and donkeys range free." (32:15-20)

When the people have reaped the full effects of their failure to trust God, when they have utterly broken their covenant with him, his response will not be to abandon them, but rather to pour out his Spirit upon them. He will not give them up. He will not abrogate his ancient promises to Abraham and his descendants. Rather, when they know their true condition, when they know the true extent of their need, he will move to meet that need. The Spirit whom they had seen at work in isolated individuals, enabling them to do what mere human abilities could not do, he will make available to everyone, to enable them to live out his character.

That this had been God's intention all along is demonstrated in the Numbers 11 passage that we looked at above. When the Spirit fell upon the elders of the Hebrew people as an expression of God's provision of additional assistance for Moses, there were two elders still in the camp. When they began to act like prophets, which had previously been the sole prerogative of Moses, the people began to get anxious and sent a messenger to the camp. This messenger told Moses what was happening and Joshua immediately spoke up and asked Moses to put a stop to this. From Moses' response, "Are you jealous for my sake?" (v. 29), it is clear that Joshua was afraid his chief's influence and authority might be diluted in some way. But Moses' further response is not only a mark of the greatness of the man, it is also a prophetic word about God's ultimate intentions and plans. Moses says, "I wish that all the LORD'S people were prophets and that the LORD would put his Spirit on them." Far from being jealous for his own prerogatives, Moses sees the need and the prospect for the meeting of that need, and longs for the day when the need will be met. He recognizes that so long as the kind of congenital refusal to trust God which is seen in the very context of this chapter (complaining about having only manna to eat) prevails, there is no way in which the goal of the covenant can be achieved. How can people who are constantly consumed with themselves ever experience unbroken fellowship with God on the basis of hearts which are wholly his? It cannot happen until the spirit of prostitution has been replaced by the Spirit of Holiness, and Moses clearly recognized this.

When we look again at Isaiah 32, we notice that the results of the Spirit's being poured out upon the people are all moral in nature. The desolation that was described in vv. 13-14 is clearly both literal and figurative, because the solution described in vv. 15-20 is both of these. Because of the people's sin, the literal land became a wasteland. War and exile depopulated the land so that there was no one to cultivate it. The great houses and defensive fortifications fell into ruins. But God's inheritance was not the land, it was the people, as is stressed again and again in the Pentateuch (e.g. Exod. 34:9; Deut. 4:20; 9:26, 29; 32:9). So it was not only the people's inheritance that was ruined and desolate, God's was as well.

So what will he do to restore his inheritance to lush fruitfulness: lives of justice and righteousness, *shalom* and trust? He will pour out the precious rainfall from heaven: his own Holy Spirit. It is certainly true that the Spirit will give power to God's people. But power for what? The doing of miracles, the manipulation of divine forces? No, it is power for living out the character of God, for treating people justly and rightly, for living lives that are whole because they are wholly God's. This is what the Spirit must do in our lives, because we cannot do it ourselves.

The same thought appears in a somewhat different context, but in similar words in Isaiah 44. Whereas chapter 32 was a call for repentance and faith, this is a call to belief and courage. But the point is the same.

> "This is what the LORD says—he who made you,
>   who formed you in the womb, and who will help you:
> Do not be afraid, O Jacob, my servant,
>   Jeshurun, whom I have chosen.
> For I will pour water on the thirsty land
>   and streams on the dry ground;
> I will pour out my Spirit on your offspring,
>   and my blessing on your descendants.
> They will spring up like grass in a meadow,
>   like poplar trees by flowing streams.
> One will say, 'I belong to the Lord';
>   another will call himself by the name of Jacob; still another
> will write on his hand, 'The LORD's,'
>   and will take the name Israel." (44:2-5)

When God's Spirit falls like rain upon his people the question of divided loyalties will no longer pertain. The Spirit will make it possible for everyone to experience the unblemished obedience and the perfect heart that only a select few in the Old Testament had experienced. Instead of that rebellious spirit which irrationally lusts after other lovers, the Holy Spirit will impart a new spirit, a new mind, which will delight itself in complete and sole identification with the Lord.

Although Jeremiah does not refer to the Spirit in his famous passage on the New Covenant, the concepts found there are the same as those in the two Isaiah passages just discussed.

> "The time is coming," declares the LORD,
>   "when I will make a new covenant
> with the house of Israel
>   and with the house of Judah.

It will not be like the covenant
　　I made with their forefathers
when I took them by the hand
　　to lead them out of Egypt,
because they broke my covenant,
　　though I was a husband to them," declares the LORD.
"This is the covenant I will make with the house of Israel
after that time," declares the LORD.
"I will put my law in their minds [Heb. "inwards"]
　　and write it on their hearts.
I will be their God,
　　and they will be my people.
No longer will a man teach his neighbor,
　　or a man his brother, saying, 'Know the LORD,'
because they will all know me,
　　from the least of them to the greatest,"
　　　　　　　　　　　　　　　　　declares the LORD.
"For I will forgive their wickedness,
and will remember their sins no more." (31:31-34)

Although there is no mention of the Holy Spirit here, the fundamental point is the same as that which we have already seen. There is no question of obeying God or not obeying God. The New Covenant will not be different in content from the Old one. If people are to be in a vital relationship with God, if they are to "know" him, then they must share his character, not merely forensically, but actually. The issue is the human heart. The Israelites broke the Old Covenant because they could not keep it in spite of their good intentions—there is something wrong with the human heart and spirit. So God can either change the content of the covenant, or he can change our hearts. It is transparently clear from this passage which of these two courses God intends to take. He will do something so that the covenant will be written in the deepest recesses of the human personality, upon our very hearts. Note how closely this parallels David's understanding of his need and the cure in Psalm 51. To be sure, this New Covenant will also have to make provision to satisfy the broken Old Covenant. Until that satisfaction is secured, the divine-human relationship is stalemated and cannot move to a new level. But

Jeremiah tells us that is exactly what will take place. In the context of the New Covenant there will be forgiveness and a Divine forgetfulness that will lose track of all our sins. But that forgiveness and forget-fulness are not so that God's people may continue in their sin and rebellion. They are in order that the Old Covenant may be set aside and the New Covenant of the Spirit might be entered into. In that New Covenant, God's people will be enabled to live for him as they could not when the covenant was external to them and not written on their hearts.

If there was any doubt about Jeremiah's view of the New Covenant as including Isaiah's views of the Spirit, that doubt is laid aside by the way in which Ezekiel incorporates both views in one. His teaching on the subject is found in chapter 36 of his book. The entire passage from v. 16 through v. 32 is important, but in the interest of space only vv. 22-28 will be quoted here.

> "Therefore say to the house of Israel, 'This is what the Sovereign Lord says: It is not for your sake, O house of Israel, that I am going to do these things, but for the sake of my holy name, which you have profaned among the nations where you have gone. I will show the holiness of my great name, which has been profaned among the nations, the name you have profaned among them. Then the nations will know that I am the Lord, declares the Sovereign Lord, when I show myself holy through you before their eyes.
>
> "For I will take you out of the nations; I will gather you from all the countries and bring you back into your own land. I will sprinkle clean water on you, and you will be clean; I will cleanse you from all your impurities and from all your idols. I will give you a new heart and put a new spirit in you; I will remove from you your heart of stone and give you a heart of flesh. And I will put my Spirit in you and move you to follow my decrees and be careful to keep my laws. You will live in the land I gave your forefathers; you will be my people, and I will be your God."[20]

---

[20]This is what Paul is talking about in 2 Cor. 2:15 in a metaphoric way. God's char-acter in us has an unmistakable aroma about it, one which is pleasant to those being saved, and one which is distinctly unpleasant to those refusing God's salvation. But in either case, the aroma is not to be missed.

What we see here is Ezekiel's explanation of Israel's situation and what God intends to do to rectify that situation. He says that Israel has been scattered to the nations because they had defiled the land with their idols. But when they had been thus scattered, they became the occasion for the Gentiles to say that Israel's God had been unable to deliver them. Thus, instead of Israel's being a witness to the nations of the incomparable holiness of the one God, she had become a cause for the nations to say that God was no more holy than their gods were. In other words, instead of hallowing the name (the reputation) of God, Israel had done the very opposite. They had been the cause of God's name being profaned (vv. 19-21). So what was God to do? Clearly he was going to have to deliver them. If he left them in captivity in Babylon, it would certainly appear that he was helpless to do anything else. So he would deliver them, but they should never think that they had somehow earned such a thing. God is doing this to show the world who he really is: the only Holy One (vv. 22-23).[21]

But what kind of deliverance would be necessary to show who God really is? Would simple restoration to the land be enough? It would not. Simply to restore his people, leaving them in the same condition that prompted the exile in the first place would accomplish very little. If God is to "show myself holy through you before their eyes" (v. 23), something much more comprehensive is going to be required.

That more comprehensive program is detailed in vv. 24-28 as quoted above. It involves four components. The first is physical deliverance (v. 24). As at the Red Sea, God must show that no earthly god can hold God's people against his will. Furthermore, God has promised the land of Canaan to his people and he, unlike the gods, is absolutely reliable. Thus, if God's unique holiness, his sole Godhood, is to be demonstrated through his people, they must be delivered from every sort of bondage. As the New Testament shows, the most

---

[21]Of course, as other texts tell us, this is not the only reason God delivered his people from exile. He also did it because he loved them and was committed to them (see Isa. 51:1-6). But the point here has to do with the evidence concerning God's nature that the Israelite people were giving before the world.

serious bondage is that to sin, death and hell. Unless we are delivered from bondage to these, then our neighbors are entirely justified in questioning whether our God is anything other than all the rest of the forces of this world claiming to be gods.

And this latter point is what prompts the further components of God's promise to his people. It is not enough that they should experience physical deliverance. They must also be enabled to demonstrate the unique character of God. For as we noted earlier, what really marks God as other than this world is his character. Of course he is utterly different in essence from his creation, a point which all the various paganisms which emphasize the continuity between gods and world fail to grasp, but in the end, it is his character which sets him apart. Thus, if God is to be shown as holy through his people, mere physical deliverance will not be enough.

The first necessity will be cleansing (v. 25). The sins of the past have left their defiling marks upon the people. The corrupt lovers of other days have left their odors clinging to God's beloved. Somehow, all of that defilement and corruption is going to have to be washed away, if we are to share intimate, loving fellowship with God. This is what David knew, and it is why he cried out so passionately for God to take a stiff brush to his very soul and make him clean again (Ps. 51:7). So God in his New Covenant with his people must make provision for restoring them to that virginal cleanness which they once knew. Ezekiel does not here specify what the method for that cleansing would be, but even without the New Testament writings, a reader knowledgeable in the Old Testament would have been able to detect its general lines. As in the great Day of Atonement when Israel's sins were cleansed and carried away, somehow God would need to provide a Sacrifice which would not merely symbolize a cleansing, but one which would actually effect such a thing. Those of us who now live in the last days know exactly how God fulfilled that promise. Through the sacrifice of Jesus Christ we have indeed been made clean from all the defilement of the sins of the past. As the writer to the Hebrews says, we may live in the presence of God with hearts that have been sprinkled to cleanse us from a guilty conscience.

But as wonderful as this promise is, it is not the fullness of the New Covenant, as is sometimes suggested in contemporary preaching. For if the people are simply restored to their land and given absolution from past sins, what is to prevent them from repeating the whole horrible story again? In fact, they will necessarily repeat that story because of the fundamental flaw in the human character that the Old Covenant exposed. Thus, if God's holiness is to be demonstrated through His people, something more than cleansing, as necessary as that is, must be done. Here Ezekiel confirms the perception of Jeremiah: there is going to have to be a change in the very thought patterns, attitudes and motivations of the people. Once, the law was written on tablets of stone and the people responded to the law out of hearts that were equally stony and hard. As a result, the law was broken again and again, and God's name was profaned because of the filthy behavior of his people.

What must happen if the law in all of its beauty is to be obeyed? Jeremiah said it must be written on our hearts, and Ezekiel says the same thing in different words. He says we must receive new hearts, hearts of tender, responsive flesh (v. 26). In place of the stubborn, self-centered will which demands that everything, including God, bow to its imperious demands, God promises us a heart which is eager and willing to do whatever God asks of us. Instead of the old rebellious spirit which prostituted itself with every false lover who presented himself, God offers a new spirit, a whole new set of attitudes which find joy in service, and delight in submission to the One it instinctively knows is a Master who does not enslave. Unless something of this sort happens, the Old Testament vision of persons who live the life of God blamelessly out of perfect hearts is a cruel joke, a moving target which is always just beyond our ability to reach it. But if indeed God can give us a new heart and a new spirit, then we can fulfill his commands, and we can find that satisfaction for which we were made—the satisfaction of genuine obedience.

But how is that new heart and spirit to be ours? What is the dynamic by which this promise is to be realized. Again, Ezekiel is in perfect consonance with his predecessors. Verse 27 spells it out. God will give us his Spirit. Just as all those great examples of the past had been able to perform superhuman feats of wisdom, craftsmanship, leadership, courage, strength, and revelation through the agency of the Holy Spirit, so we shall be empowered for superhuman feats of obedience through the same Holy Spirit. And it is important to note that just as Isaiah emphasized, Ezekiel says the gift of the Spirit will be primarily for feats of moral achievement. Because the Spirit of God is within us, our will will be oriented towards God's will and not away from it. Because the Spirit of God is within us, our delight will be obedience and not disobedience. Because the Spirit of God is within us, living his life will not be an alien thing that we do with difficulty and struggle; rather, it will be our native air.

In Ezekiel 37, this truth is put into pictures. The prophet is taken into a terrible valley. Some great slaughter has taken place here, and the bodies have been left to decay where they fell. Now the whole valley is covered with desiccated bones. This is a picture of Israel. All the bright hopes that gathered around the foot of Sinai are gone. The nation is dead, strangers in a strange land, doomed to disappear into the vast homogenous mass that the world-empires sponsored in order to keep order. Their religion would be absorbed into the common syncretized religion of the times, and the witness to the only truly Holy One would be lost. And yet God asks Ezekiel if he thinks the dry bones can live. Ezekiel wisely defers to God on that question. God says the bones can live, that they will be covered with tendons and flesh again. Sure enough, that is what happens. At Ezekiel's word the bodies are reformed before his eyes. But there is no breath (remember that "breath," "wind," and "spirit" are the same word in Hebrew). So Ezekiel speaks again, and a breath comes from the four winds and the bodies come to life.

What is the meaning of this bizarre picture? It is explained in vv. 12-14.

> "Therefore prophesy and say to them: 'This is what the Sovereign LORD says: O my people, I am going to open your graves and bring you up from them; I will bring you back to the land of Israel. Then you, my people will know that I am the LORD, when I open your graves and bring you up from them. I

will put my Spirit in you and you will live, and I will settle you in your own land. Then you will know that I the LORD have spoken, and I have done it.'"

In other words, this is the same point that was made in a more didactic way in chapter 36. It would not be enough for the nation to be reborn, miraculous as that would be. No, something more would need to take place if the original purpose of the Exodus was really to be fulfilled. If Israel is really to know who Yahweh (the LORD) is, if they are truly to be his people, and he their God, then God's own life-breath must take up residence in them. Whatever else their experience should have taught them, it was this: in themselves they were helpless to live the life of God which God called upon them to live. But there was something else God wished to teach them. What was not achievable by human might or by human power was achievable through the Spirit of God (see Zech. 4:7).

This is the New Covenant, as the Hebrew prophets predicted it. To suggest, as too many do today, that the New Covenant differs from the Old by offering forgiveness in place of demanding obedience is a sad travesty. The New Covenant demands obedience every bit as strongly as does the Old one, as will be confirmed in our study of the New Testament in later chapters. But this truth is already made clear even in the Old Testament predictions, as we have seen. The difference between the two covenants is not in content. In both cases God offers himself to us without reservation and, on the basis of his prior gracious deliverance, invites us to give ourselves to him in exclusive and total commitment. The terms of that commitment are lives that reflect both in breadth and depth the character of God, and in particular, self-giving love. That is the content of the Old Covenant and that is the content of the New Covenant. The Old Covenant does not suggest that we can enter into a relationship with God through our obedience, and the New does not suggest that if we accept the sacrifice of Christ obedience, while desirable, is not really necessary.

So what is the difference between the two covenants? The difference is precisely where Jeremiah and Ezekiel place it. The Old Covenant was external. It stood over against the worshipper and, as such, it showed him or her in no uncertain terms who God was, and who he or she was. The Old Covenant called for an obedience that the worshipper discovered was not only beyond his or her ability, it was, more frighteningly, beyond his or her desire. So was the Old Covenant a failure? Not at all! It was profoundly successful. It drove the righteous remnant of Israel to their knees where they cried out for God to do something for them. What did they ask God to do? They asked him to cleanse them from their filthiness and enable them to live in the way that their minds told them was the only way to live (see below on Romans, chapter 7). In other words, as Paul says, the Old Covenant was a schoolmaster to bring us to Christ.

The New Covenant differs from the Old in this one respect. It is internal. Because of Christ's sacrifice, the temple of our heart and spirit can be cleansed from the sins of the past and the Spirit can take up residence within us. Now God's will can function from within us; now his nature can flow out of us. Now what was once an unattainable goal becomes a living reality. This is what the Old Testament teaches and what the New Testament confirms.

There is one more Old Testament passage concerning the Holy Spirit that sheds an important light upon this discussion. This is the one in Joel 2, made famous by Peter's reference to it on the Day of Pentecost:

> "And afterward,
> I will pour out my Spirit on all people.
> Your sons and daughters will prophesy,
> your old men will dream dreams,
> your young men will see visions.
> Even on my servants, both men and women,
> I will pour out my Spirit in those days....
>
> And everyone who calls
> on the name of the LORD will be saved;
> for on Mount Zion and in Jerusalem
> there will be deliverance,
> as the LORD has said,
> among the survivors
> whom the LORD calls." (2:28-29, 32)

For our purposes here the chief significance of this passage is the confirmation that God intends to make the gift of the Spirit universal. He had demonstrated the need for, and the possibility of, Spirit-enablement with a chosen few. And Moses had hinted at the possibility that the gift could be for all when he expressed the wish that all God's people could be filled with the Spirit. Now the hints and the hopes are met with positive affirmation. The all-inclusive nature of the promise could hardly be expressed more forcefully. Everyone may receive the Spirit of God: gender is no barrier; age is no barrier; class is no barrier. Neither is nationality, because the passage begins with the statement that God will pour His Spirit upon "all flesh" [NIV all people]. "Flesh" admits of no exclusions at all. It is God's intent that everybody, everywhere be filled with the Holy Spirit in order that they may share his life walking in obedience with him. This is the heart of the message of the Old Testament.

6

The Spirit and the Messiah

What was the means by which the promised Holy Spirit would come upon the people of God? Before Jesus left the earth in his ascension, he made a rather enigmatic statement which gives us a clue to the answer to that question. He told the disciples to wait for "the promise of the Father" (Luke 24:49). Interestingly, the apostles raised no questions about this statement. This was not their normal approach when Jesus said things, even things which seem quite clear to us. Very often they had questions to ask. So Jesus said, "You know where I am going," and they responded, "We have no idea where you are going." So we might expect them to say in this case, "What promise of the Father?" But they do not. Why? Is it possible that in this case Jesus had for once said something that they expected the Messiah to say? So many times Jesus had said things that they had never expected a Messiah to say, and they were confused and upset. But here, they seem to accept the enigmatic saying with no trouble. This suggests that the statement was not enigmatic to them, that indeed, it was quite intelligible to them on the Messiah's lips.

This possibility seems quite likely when we discover that the Old Testament prophecies of the Messiah show a special intimacy between his mission and the promised pouring out of the Holy Spirit upon all flesh. In fact, we might go so far as to say that except for Isaiah 53 the connection between the Messiah and the giving of the Holy Spirit is considerably clearer in the Old Testament than is his atoning death and resurrection. This is not to suggest in any way that these emphases are not present in the Old Testament, but it is simply to say that sometimes modern Christian teaching makes primary what the Old Testament does not.

In this regard, it is most interesting to see how John the Baptist characterized the ministry of the Messiah when he was asked if he was that person. In all four Gospels the same point is made. This is significant since the Gospel of John only repeats what is found in the other three Gospels in about 10 percent of the cases. When John does repeat what they say, we may safely assume that the point is considered to be of great importance. In this case, John the Baptist says that the difference between the Messiah and himself is that he baptizes with water while the Messiah will baptize with the Holy Spirit (Matt. 3:11; Mark 1:8; Luke 3:16; John 1:33). What would the average Christian say was the purpose of Jesus' coming into the world? Almost certainly they would not say what John said. We would be much more likely to say that he came to die for our sins. To be sure, he did come for that purpose. The Gospel of John also has John the Baptist saying, "Look, the Lamb of God, who takes away the sin of the world" (1:29). But Jesus' atoning death was an intermediate goal, not the ultimate one. When John thought of the Messiah and his function in the world, his first thought was that he came to give the Holy Spirit to people. He was certainly confirmed in that thought by God's revelation to him as reported in John 1:33:

> I would not have known him, except that the one who sent me
> to baptize with water told me, 'The man on whom you see the
> Spirit come down and remain is he who will baptize with the
> Holy Spirit.'

The atoning sacrifice was necessary in order to cleanse the temple in which the Holy Spirit would reside, but that sacrifice was not an end in itself. It was a means to a greater end, an end the Old Testament believers had looked forward to with breathless anticipation: the hour when God would fill all his people with himself and enable them to live out his holy life.

This explains why the symbolic baptism was so important to Jesus. John was certainly right when he said that it would be more appropriate for Jesus to baptize John than the reverse (Matt. 3:14), but Jesus said that this would fulfill what was right (v. 15). Why was this right? Because the Old Testament prophecies of the Messiah make it clear that the Messiah is himself a man upon whom the Spirit rests, but also that the life of the Spirit will uniquely characterize his ministry. In fact, the passage from Isaiah which Jesus used to introduce his ministry and to validate his claim to Messiahship is the most explicit upon this point:

> The Spirit of the Sovereign LORD is on me,
>   because the LORD has anointed me
>   to preach good news to the poor.
> He has sent me to bind up the broken-hearted,
>   to proclaim freedom for the captives
>   and release from darkness for the prisoners,
> to proclaim the year of the LORD's favor
>   and the day of vengeance of our God,
> to comfort all who mourn,
>   and provide for those who grieve in Zion—
> to bestow on them a crown of beauty
>   instead of ashes,
> the oil of gladness
>   instead of mourning,
> and a garment of praise
>   instead of a spirit of despair.
> They will be called oaks of righteousness,
>   a planting of the LORD for the display of his splendor.
>   (Isa. 61:1-3; Luke 4:18-19)

The premier mark of the Messiah was that he was a man upon whom the Spirit rested and through whom he proclaimed the message of hope and a new life of righteousness. Of course Jesus as the second person of the Trinity did not need to be filled with the Holy

Spirit. But he did need to confirm his messiahship through a visible indication of that Spirit-anointing and Spirit-empowering. This is why John's testimony in John 1:32-33 is so important. He can say to the world, "Yes, Jesus is the promised Messiah who will dispense God's Spirit. I know it because I have seen the Spirit come upon him."

But if Isaiah 61:1-3 by itself shows the unmistakable link between the Messiah and the Holy Spirit, it is far from the only Old Testament statement of this link. This is especially the case with the Messianic prophecies in Isaiah. Again and again the prophet makes it clear that the work of the Messiah will be inseparable from that of the Spirit. Not only will the Spirit be particularly manifest in the Messiah and his reign, that reign will be one in which the Spirit will be poured out upon the earth.

The prophecy found in Isaiah 11:2 states that the Messiah's reign will be marked by the Spirit's presence and empowerment.

> The Spirit of the LORD will rest on him—
> the Spirit of wisdom and of understanding,
> the Spirit of counsel and of power,
> the Spirit of knowledge and of the fear of the LORD—

Unlike Ahaz and many of the other Davidic monarchs whose reigns were marked by another spirit altogether, the true Branch from Jesse would show the real meaning of wise counsel, and the true meaning of power, a power born out of an intimate knowledge of God. In him the revelation of the Spirit of God would be complete.

Although the Spirit is not mentioned in the description of the Davidic messiah in 16:5, all the characteristics which we have seen to be associated with the life of the Spirit are portrayed there.

> In *love* a throne will be established;
> in *faithfulness* a man will sit on it—
> one from the house of David—
> one who in judging seeks *justice*
> and speeds the cause of *righteousness*.

These qualities are the result of Spirit-empowerment and the Messiah will demonstrate them in their completeness.

In chapter 32 there is an interesting conjunction of ideas which again points to the importance of the Spirit in the Messiah's ministry. In vv. 1-8 there is a description of the unique behavior of those in the Messiah's kingdom. The King and his rulers will rule in justice and righteousness (v. 1). Instead of the strong devouring those weaker than they, the strong will become shelters and refuges for the weak (v. 2). Eyes which had been blind, ears which had been deaf, hearts which had been insensitive, and tongues which had been dumb (cf. ch. 6) will all be opened to see, hear, understand, and witness (vv. 3-4). Wicked fools will be seen for what they really are, while those who are truly free (*n^ediba*, "noble" NIV, see the discussion above) will be recognized and honored as such (vv. 5-8).

This segment is followed by a denunciation of complacency (vv. 9-13). It is not clear whether this is a complacency engendered by the preceding promises, or by some hopeful circumstances in the world around. In the general context of chapters 28-39, which seem to reflect the events of 710-701 B.C., it is possible that the momentary relaxation of the Assyrian pressure mentioned in 37:8 was the cause of the complacency. But in any case, the contrast is clear: it is between God's kingdom where a completely new ethic and behavior will be seen, and "business as usual" in which it is thought that human effort and ability will be enough. In fact, as Isaiah shows, human effort and ability will not be enough. They will result in a desolate land and ruined cities.

So how will the Messiah's kingdom come to pass? Verses 14-20, which we considered above, answers that question. The characteristic qualities of the Messiah's kingdom will be the result of the outpouring of the Spirit. The spiritual abundance, the justice and righteousness, the peace and spiritual freedom, the renewed ability to trust God, all this will take place because the Spirit is poured out. Thus, although the Spirit is not mentioned directly in the description of the Messianic kingdom in 32:1-8, the larger context of the passage shows that there is an intimate connection between that kingdom and the giving of the Spirit.

The connection is made explicit again in 42:1-7 in the first of the four so-called "Suffering Servant" passages.[22] God says that his Servant will bring justice and righteousness to the world in "faithfulness"(vv. 1-3). Furthermore, he will be "a covenant to the people and a light for the Gentiles" (v. 6), opening the eyes of the blind, and freeing captives from prison (v. 7). Although many contemporary scholars wish to deny this and the other "Suffering Servant" passages to the Messiah, it cannot help but be obvious that these are the very same things which have been said of the Messiah both earlier and later in the book. But the key point for us here is almost the very first statement in the passage,

> Here is my servant, whom I uphold
> my chosen one in whom I delight;
> I will put my Spirit on him,
> and he will bring justice to the nations. (v. 1)

How will the Servant, the Messiah, bring justice to the nations? Through the Spirit who rests upon him! The Messiah's blessed ministry to the world will be a ministry of the Spirit of God. In this context, it is worth noting the similar language used here and at Jesus' baptism. When the Spirit of God descended upon Jesus, a voice from heaven said, "This is my Son, whom I love; with him I am well pleased" (Matt. 3:17). The words "with him I am well-pleased" represent the Greek words which are an exact translation of the Hebrew translated here "in whom I delight." Here we have a further revelation of who this "chosen one" is; he is God's own Son. But the link to the Old Testament messiah is perfectly clear. He is the one who

---

[22]The other three are found in 49:1-7; 50:4-9; and 52:13-53:12. For much of this century the prevailing opinion was that these were originally four independent pieces which had been interleaved into the book at these points. That opinion is now changing and more scholars are willing to see the four pieces as integral to chapters 40-55 whenever they think this section was first written.

completely pleases God, the one on whom the Spirit of God rests in his fullness.

All of this is brought to its culmination in 61:1-3 which we have already looked at: the Messiah has been anointed by the Father with the Spirit for the purpose of carrying out his ministry; one which will culminate in the people of God being able to live the righteous lives to which both the Old and the New Covenants call them.[23]

But perhaps it will be said that this connection between the Spirit and the ministry of the Messiah is limited to the prophecies of Isaiah. While this is true, it is also true that the vast majority of Old Testament prophecies of the Messiah are to be found in Isaiah. Take these away and the number of prophecies of the Messiah is much smaller. But beyond this, the very connections which the Gospels draw confirm the significance of what Isaiah says. The Messiah's ministry is made possible through the Holy Spirit and his ministry is one which makes the promises of the giving of the Holy Spirit in the Old Testament realizable.

---

[23]There is an enigmatic reference in 59:21 which it is tempting to add to the Messiah/Spirit collection in Isaiah. The preceding vv. (59:15b-20) clearly describe the Messiah's defeat of the forces which have rendered it impossible for his people to live lives of justice and righteousness (a condition described in vv. 59:1-15a). Then v. 21 says, "'As for me, this is my covenant with them,' says the LORD. 'My Spirit who is on you, and my words that I have put in your mouth, will not depart from your mouth, or from the mouths of your children or from the mouths of their descendants from this time on and forever,' says the LORD." The problem with the passage is to try to sort out to whom "you" refers. Is it the Messiah? Then who are his "children" and "descendants"? If it could be maintained that these are his followers the supposition might stand, but since that is not clear, it is perhaps better to suppose that the reference is to Isaiah himself. At any rate, this is another place where the presence of the Spirit and the living of a righteous life are intimately connected in the OT.

7

The Old Testament and Holiness

Before we turn to see how all this theology of holiness is worked out in the New Testament, let me summarize what I have said thus far. The Old Testament teaches us that God's goal for human life is that we should live in fellowship with him. But fundamental to such fellowship is both proper understanding and proper character. No true relationship is possible unless the parties understand each other correctly and unless they have common goals and concerns. So it is with God and us. If we try to treat God as though he were identical with the world—to be manipulated through the world by our efforts, a source of power for the achievement of our goals—fellowship is impossible. For God is not of this world and he will not be manipulated through it. Because of these facts, he is the only one who can rightly be called "holy." He is the only one who is truly Other, which is at the heart of the idea of "holy." Thus, fellowship with him is only possible if we renounce at the outset all attempts to manipulate him. In fact, there is only one way to receive the blessings he wants to pour out on us: absolute renunciation of all efforts to control him and complete surrender to him.

Not only does fellowship with God require correct understanding of God and his relationship to the world, it also requires a sharing of his character. As Amos 3:3 says, "How can two walk together, unless they are agreed?" Thus, the covenant was the statement of the character of God which the people would need to replicate if they were to walk with him. It was not merely a set of arbitrary laws that a tyrannical deity forced upon people to bend them to his will. Rather, it was a means of teaching this spiritually-backward people what the Divine character really was. And since this is the character of the Creator of the universe, there is an inherent rightness in the character of these commands that we creatures recognize when we allow ourselves to. So obedience to the commands would be a means of participating in the holy character of God. We cannot be transcendent as he is transcendent, but we can be loving as he is loving, faithful as he is faithful, and pure as he is pure. Thus when the covenant calls the people to be holy, it is neither calling them to some metaphysical impossibility, nor is it calling them to mere exclusive relationship. It is calling them to an exclusive relationship that will issue in a changed behavior.

But if the covenant served to teach the people the character of God as it called them to live out his life, it also taught them their own character. For although they thought that living God's life was merely a matter of their deciding to do so, they quickly discovered this was not the case. They discovered in themselves a positive predilection *not* to live God's life. To the more thoughtful among them, this was profoundly puzzling, because not only had they sworn with the most terrible oaths to obey these commands, the commands had about them an inherent rightness which made obeying them quite sensible. Nor were the commands obscure and difficult. As Moses said in Deuteronomy 10:12-13, "All God is asking us to do is to fear him, walk in his ways, and love him with all we are by keeping these commands." Clearly, Moses' implied question is "That's not so hard, is it?"

And by all rights, that shouldn't be hard. Yet the Israelites found it impossibly hard. Try as they might they found themselves chasing after other gods who seemed to promise power, comfort, pleasure, and security without the onerous call for exclusive obedience and total surrender. They found themselves oppressing one another in the scrabble for power and prestige. They found themselves deifying their own sexuality in an attempt to gain control of the forces of life. In the end they were forced to recognize that there is a flaw in the human spirit. There is something in us which predisposes us to the perverse rather than the true, to the evil rather than the good, to the dark rather than the light.

So what is the Old Testament response to all of this? Is it simply to admit that we have reached an impasse? Is God's goal simply to bring us to the point of understanding that although he demands we live lives like his, we cannot, and that is all there is to the matter? Not at all. We saw that it was possible for Old Testament believers to live lives which were blameless in God's sight out of hearts which were undivided in their devotion to him. Furthermore, we saw how the Old Testament writers assessed the nature both of the problem and of the cure. What they came to realize is that this flaw in the human character can be said to reside in our "spirits," in that which motivates us, which expresses our attitudes and patterns of behavior. Thus, if we are to live the life of God as he expects, something must be done in our spirits. There must be a "new spirit" in us. That is, there must be a fundamental change in our attitudes, motives, and patterns of response. There must be a change from a stubborn "I"-centered response to a malleable, God-centered one. And what the Old Testament believers came to realize was that such a change is only possible if God himself effects the change by giving us an infusion of his own Spirit.

Thus, the Old Testament closes with two conflicting emotions. On the one hand, there is the sinking note of despair. In spite of their marvelous revelation which God had so kindly given them, and in spite of their long history which should have taught them something, they seemed to be no nearer God than ever. True, their faith had survived the fires of the Exile, but to what? The pictures in Ezra and Nehemiah are profoundly discouraging. Faithfulness to their covenant and love for each other seem to be no more a part of the people's lives than they had been 1000 years before. And if we read the history of the intertestamental period (400-1 B.C.) there are hardly any grounds for more encouragement. To be sure, there is a growing commitment to keep the letter of the law, and there is a growing hatred of idolatry, but the picture of national life with its selling of the priesthood and the dynastic bloodletting among its rulers and kings is not at all promising.

At the same time the Old Testament closes on a rising note of hope. Surely God had not brought them all this way to leave them in their sin and despair now. Surely that long history of promise and fulfillment could not end like this. God *was* the King of the whole universe and surely he would make his kingdom manifest in the world. God's covenant was the way of life and surely he would bring that covenant to it fulfillment. He had promised to pour out his Spirit on all flesh in the last days and usher in a new era of justice and righteousness in which his people *would* be able to live the life he called them to. The true anointed one (Messiah) would appear, a king who would care more for his people than he did for himself. He would be the messenger of the covenant, who would purify his people with fire. He would make God's Spirit available to all, and the promises of Isaiah 60-62 would become a reality.

Perhaps the conflict of these emotions of despair and hope is one of the factors accounting for the unusual excitability of the Jewish people at the time of Christ. Certainly they contributed to the intense factionalism which characterized Judaism at this point. Each group knew exactly how the hope was going to replace the despair, and they were immediately ready to destroy any other group that opposed them. Of course the events of the previous 100 years, with the disintegration of the native Hasmonean dynasty, the endless intrigues for the high priesthood, and the coming of the Romans were factors as well. But the constant shuttling between despair and hope must have contributed also.

It was into this welter of emotion, violence, intrigue, hope, and despair that the Son of God stepped. He came, as he said, to bring all of the Old Testament promises to their fulfillment. How he did that was a shock and a surprise to many, and yet when we look at the New Testament in the light of what we have just seen of the Old Testament, we will see a consonance between the two parts of the Bible that has all too often been ignored in the history of biblical interpretation.

PART TWO

THE NEW TESTAMENT

8

The New Covenant and the Holy Life

At several points in the previous pages, I have spoken of the unfortunate suggestion which has arisen at various times in the Church that there is a fundamental difference in the modes of salvation in the Old Testament and the New. Normally those who have taught or written on these subjects have made their points with careful qualification so that adequate attention is given to the fundamental similarities between the teachings of the two testaments. But in the course of transmission throughout the Church these qualifications tend to get lost or obscured until it is made to appear that the differences are quite radical.

Thus, it is all too common today for people to believe that in the Old Testament the Israelites were reconciled to God on the basis of their obedience to the Law, while Christians are reconciled to him solely by grace through faith in the atoning death of Christ. Neither of these views is correct. In fact, as argued above, the people of the Old Testament were brought into a relationship with God by an acceptance of grace. Paul makes this point forcefully in regard to Abraham in Galatians chapter 3. But he could have continued the point as regards the descendants of Jacob. They did not come into a relationship with God by their obedience to the covenant. God delivered them from Egypt by an act of sheer grace. It is only after they are in that delivered relationship that God reveals the terms of a continued relationship: the covenant. As we said above, the way to God is grace; the walk with God is obedience.

The same situation applies in the New Testament. There is nothing we can do to save ourselves. We are slaves to sin, and are helpless to free ourselves. We are under a just condemnation, and there is nothing we can do to escape it. If we are to be restored to a condition of innocence in which we can enjoy fellowship with the Holy God, it will be by his grace alone. But having been restored by his grace, he requires that we shall live a life like his. John says we cannot be simultaneously in the dark and in the light (1 John. 1:5-6). We cannot live lives of sin and enjoy fellowship with the Sinless One.

But how can we, sinners that we are, ever do anything but live lives of sin? John not only makes the statement just quoted, he also says that if we say we are without sin, we lie (1 John 1:8)! The answer to the question is the same as it is in the Old Testament—through the infilling of the Holy Spirit. In the previous chapter we noted that it was expected that one of the things the Messiah would do would be to make the Holy Spirit available to all. In fact, we saw that to John the Baptist, this giving of the Spirit would be the single most important aspect of the Messiah's ministry. His whole ministry could be subsumed under the single head: "He will baptize with the Holy Spirit." Thus when Jesus told the disciples to wait in Jerusalem after his ascension for "the promise of the Father," this occasioned no comment from them. Of course, his comments about the Spirit in his so-called "Last Supper Discourse" (John 13-17, discussed below) also prepared them for that statement. Nevertheless, they seem to have understood that the culmination of Christ's ministry and the beginning of theirs would not occur until the Holy Spirit had been given.

So the New Testament exhibits the same pattern for relating to God as does the Old Testament: (1) we come into the relationship solely by receiving God's grace; (2) to be in the relationship requires that we manifest Christ's character; (3) but we cannot do this in our own strength; (4) therefore it is necessary for us to rely entirely upon the Holy Spirit who reproduces Christ's character in us.

Nowhere is this pattern seen more clearly in a brief compass than in Paul's letter to the Romans. Some have thought that Paul may have planned it in advance as a summary of Christian theology, because more than any other of his letters, it shows clear logical organization from start to finish. In the first five chapters, he shows the necessity of faith in God's gracious provision in Christ. In chapters six through eight, he shows what the life implications of such a faith are, and how emerging Judaism was missing the truth of the revelation. This necessitates his showing that the promises of God to the Hebrew people are not nullified by Christ but will be confirmed in him (chaps. 9-11). Finally, Paul shows what kind of behavior the transformed life will issue in (chaps. 12-15).

It is particularly in chapters 6 through 8 that the fundamental similarity with the Old Testament becomes clearest, so I want to look at those in some detail. Chapters 1-5 show in no uncertain terms that no one can stand before God protesting their innocence. The only way we can survive in his presence is through faith in Jesus, the way of escape provided by God. In the first chapter he shows that the Gentiles knew enough of God not to become idolators, and yet they did and in consequence have sunk to the most despicable sins. But in chapters two and three, he shows that the Jews have no cause for self-congratulation. If anything, their situation is worse because they have the written revelation and are thus responsible for their greater knowledge. But this greater knowledge has not resulted in the kind of obedience it should. For with their minds and their mouths the Jews commend the Law, all the while failing to live up to what they know. Thus Paul can say towards the end of chapter 3, "All have sinned and fall short of the glory of God" (v. 23).

So what is the answer? If all humans stand condemned before God, and if there is nothing we can do to clear the charges from our record, what can we do? Paul begins to answer this question already in chapter 3, beginning at v. 21. God has made his righteousness available to us through faith in the atoning sacrifice of Christ. He goes on to flesh out this assertion in chapters 4 and 5. He shows that the law was never given as a source by which humans might make themselves right before God. Long before the law was given, Abraham was justified by faith (4:13), and the Law is unable to deal with the sinful inclinations which have been ours since our first parents sinned (5:12-14). Rather, the function of the Law was to show us just how sinful we are (5:20-21) and thus prepare us for the Cross.

Thus, if the reader has followed Paul carefully through these first five chapters, he or she has gotten a strong dose of a single idea: there is nothing I ever did or ever could do which would make me worthy of the love of God in Christ Jesus. That love is a free gift given to me by God in the helplessness and the hopelessness of my sin. Whether I am a Gentile or a Jew, I am incapable of earning any standing with God through my actions. Right standing with him is only possible because Christ has died for my sins. My only choice is either to accept or reject what Christ has done for me.

Do Not Sin

From one point of view, we might think that the book could end here. After all, Paul has given his readers the gospel, has he not? We are saved by grace through faith alone. We are the heirs of heaven, forgiven of our sins, no longer under condemnation. What more is there? Fortunately, there is a great deal more to the Good News than that, and Paul launches into it in chapter 6. Throughout the book he uses a dialogical style of writing. That is, he anticipates the questions and comments of an imaginary hearer and writes to address these. Here the question is a fairly obvious one in the light of the stress that Paul has given thus far to the worthlessness of our good deeds. Here the imaginary hearer says something like this: "I understand your point, Paul. Nothing I ever did made me acceptable to God. In fact, my righteousness is filthy and vile, because it is just self-serving. Actually my 'goodness' was probably a barrier to finding Christ because it made me think I didn't need him. So, if that's true; if none of my good deeds made me acceptable to God, and if they actually kept me from God, then it doesn't matter how I live now that I have accepted God's offer of Christ. In fact, if I just surrender to my sins, Christ will be free to give more of the grace he so much enjoys giving!"

To all of this, Paul goes off like a rocket. It is interesting to see the various translations of his explosion, which is literally, "May it never be!" (NASB). The Authorized Version has the familiar "God forbid!" while the New International Version and the New Revised Standard Version have "By no means!" The New King James Version says "Certainly not!" and the Jerusalem Bible says "Of course not!" The New English Bible has simply "No, no!" All of these are reflecting Paul's horror over such a thought. The very idea that Christians might think that they should just go on living in sin after they had received Christ's forgiveness is abhorrent to the apostle. And when it is stated baldly like this, few Christians would want to argue for such a point of view. But in practice, all too many today accept this as a modus operandi. Yes, we should fight against sin as much as we can. But even while we are fighting it, we know that we cannot help but fall into it. So we need just to live in the awareness of our forgiven-ness and not make too many great pretensions.

But Paul will have none of this, and we can understand why when we think of his background. Paul is a child of the Old Testament and is thinking like an Old Testament believer (which is not the same as thinking like a Jew). Why did God deliver his people from Egypt? So that they could live like pagan Egyptians, but with a good conscience? Never! Well then, he delivered them so that he could fulfill his promise to give them a land of their own. That is certainly closer to the truth, but if so, why the covenant? If God's ultimate purpose for his people was merely to give them a land, the covenant seems quite superfluous. No, God's purpose in delivering his people from Egypt was the same as his purpose for calling Abraham. It was in order that humans might share his divine character. So Paul says here, "Don't you understand? Why did Jesus give his life for you—just so that he could stamp 'justified' on you? Never! He did it so that he could stamp his image on you!"

This is then the theme of the entire sixth chapter: you must not sin. From start to finish it is a commandment. But perhaps someone will say, "Oh, I quite agree with you. God never wants us to sin, and as Christians we should never be happy about our sinning, but that does not mean we can do anything but sin." But that mistakes the nature of a commandment. A commandment assumes the possibility of compliance. Imagine that we are in a tall building and we suddenly see someone falling past an open window. So I shout out the window at the person falling, "Don't hit the sidewalk!" What would you think? At best you would think I had lost my mind. That person cannot help but hit the sidewalk, and it is foolish, if not cruel, to say such a thing to them. Or suppose someone has been awake for 48 hours and now they sit down in a warm room at 1:00 p.m. after a big lunch to listen to a lecture on the Hebrew verb, and I tell them, "Don't go to sleep." I might as well save my breath. Even if the person has a vital interest in the subject and sincerely tries to stay awake, they *will* go to sleep. They cannot obey my command and it is foolish for me to expect that they will obey it.

But Paul seems to have no misgivings about demanding in the strongest terms that his hearers not engage in sin. He gives three reasons for this demand. First of all, he says that we need not sin. In verses 2b through 7, he says the following:

> We died to sin; how can we live in it any longer? Or don't you know that all of us who were baptized into Christ Jesus were baptized into his death? We were therefore buried with him through baptism into death in order that, just as Christ was raised from the dead through the glory of the Father, we too may live a new life. If we have been united with him like this in his death, we will certainly also be united with him in his resurrection. For we know that our old self was crucified with him so that the body of sin might be rendered powerless, that we should no longer be slaves to sin—because anyone who has died has been freed from sin.

Paul's point here is that through our identification with Christ, his death to sin and his resurrection to new life are ours. So when we died with Christ, we died to sin. And when we rose from the dead with Christ we rose to new life, a life that did not include sin. Why were we justified? So that we "may live a new life." Nor is that merely figurative, because "our old self was crucified with him so that the body of sin might be "rendered powerless." Is that merely forensic? Is Paul merely saying that Christ died so that our record could be clean, while in fact we continued to sin? Not at all, for the rest of the sentence says, "that we should no longer be slaves to sin."

Paul is speaking here of one of the most glorious truths of the Christian faith, the identification of the believer with the risen Christ. Among the several distinguishing features of Christianity from the other religions of the world, this one is perhaps the most wonderful. Our founder is alive! Buddha is dead; Mohammed is dead; Confucius is dead; the founders of Hinduism and Shinto are dead; Moses is dead. But Jesus is alive. And the miracle of being a Christian is "Christ in you." Christianity is not primarily a set of ideas to which we give intellectual assent. Christianity is not primarily a moral code to which we agree. Christianity is not primarily a set of ethical standards to which we adhere. Christianity is a life that has been crucified in Christ and is continually resurrected by his resurrection power in us.[24] So Paul says, "Go on in sin? How could you think that? You have been resurrected with Christ? How could you continue to sin?"

But not only does Paul say we need not sin because we have been identified with Christ, he goes further to say we *must* not sin. Here he is speaking of the addictive power of sin. In verses 13 and 14 he says "Do not offer the parts of your body to sin, as instruments of wicked-ness, but rather offer yourselves to God…. For sin shall not be your master." What he is saying is that sin is an either/or proposition. You cannot be a little bit sinful anymore than you can be a little bit pregnant. Either you are or you aren't. So Paul is saying that if we give our bodies to sin, then sin is our master. Sin will gain control of us, and in its addictive power, will draw us back into its coils so that we are unable to live the life of Christ.

---

[24]This is another way of speaking about the reality of being filled with the Holy Spirit which we will discuss further below.

But someone says, "It is not that I plan to sin, or even want to, I just do it. Surely Paul is talking about someone who *wants* to sin here." But Paul's point does not have to do with what we want to do or don't want to do. He is simply saying that if we engage in sin, then it is our master. Sin is telling us what to do, and Christ is not.

> Don't you know that when you offer yourselves to someone to obey him as slaves, you are slaves to the one whom you obey— whether you are slaves to sin, which leads to death, or to obedience, which leads to righteousness? But thanks be to God that, though you used to be slaves to sin, you wholeheartedly obeyed the form of teaching to which you were entrusted. You have been set free from sin and have become slaves to righteousness (vv. 16-18).

As Jesus says, we cannot serve two masters (Matt. 6:24). So Paul says that we must not sin because it is addictive. To open any door to it is to deny the new mastery that we accepted when we accepted Christ.

But Paul gives another reason why we must not sin. This is because we are the Bride of Christ. While he does not use that precise term here, this is one of the clear implications of the statement "offer the parts of your body to him as instruments of righteousness. For sin shall not be your master [just] because you are not under law, but under grace." Imagine this picture. Sitting on a curb along the street of a great city is a woman dressed in rags. Her hair hangs in greasy strings. Her skin seems impregnated with dirt. She stares around her with insolent eyes. Suddenly there is a flourish of trumpets. Around a corner comes the gilded carriage of the prince of that kingdom. He is a handsome young man of power and grace and all the princesses of the surrounding kingdoms have set their caps for him. As the carriage passes the spot where the woman is sitting, the prince suddenly calls out to the driver, "Stop!" As the carriage slides to a stop, the prince says to one of the footmen, "Do you see that woman? That's the woman I want to marry. Ask her if she is willing, and if she will come to live in the palace until our wedding day can be arranged."

Now the scene shifts. We go to the palace on the wedding day. We are in the bride's chamber. And what do we see? There sits the bride cross-legged in the middle of the beautiful bed stuffing her mouth with candy. She is still in her rags; her hair still hangs down in greasy strings; her skin is still the color of earth. Around her are the ladies-in-waiting with the gown, the soaps, and the perfumes. At one side is the hairdresser. One of the ladies finally says hesitantly, "My lady, don't—don't you want to get ready?" But the woman's answer comes out harshly through her full mouth. "He liked me well enough when I was sitting in the gutter like this, so I guess he can marry me like this, too."

Yes, there was nothing I did to deserve his love. He saw me in the gutter, in my rags, and in my filth, and he said, "I love you. You are my bride." So what will I say? Will I say, "Well, rags were good enough for him in the beginning. I guess they will be good enough for him all the way." Never! Rather I will say, "Oh, don't you have some stronger soap? I need something that will get all this grime and grease off me. Don't you have a wire brush I can use on my fingernails? And that is lovely perfume, but don't you have something even more elegant? He deserves the best! How he could have ever loved me I don't know, but today I will be all I can be for him." Everyone else looking at her said, "What a worthless wench." But the Prince saw his bride. Shall we persist in our rags, our grime—our sins? Not at all! Paul says, "Thanks be to God that, though you used to be slaves to sin, you whole-heartedly obeyed the form of teaching to which you were entrusted. You have been set free from sin and have become slaves to righteousness" (vv. 17-18). We must not sin, because we cannot return again to the slavery of sin when he has called us his bride.

But Paul goes yet further. Not only do we need not sin, and we must not sin, we *dare* not sin. For the wages of sin is death (v. 23). This verse is frequently learned as one of a series in the so-called Plan of Salvation. So we quote it to persons when we are encouraging them to turn from sin and accept Christ. But as valid as the statement may be in that context, Paul is not using it in that way here. Here he is writing to the believer. Why can we Christians not continue in sin? Because the wages of sin is death! You cannot earn eternal life, that is a gift from God. But you can earn eternal death if you continue in sin after supposedly accepting Christ's offer. Thus, Paul has saved his most chilling argument until the end of the chapter. He says that the reason a Christian cannot continue in sin so that Christ's grace may abound is that you cannot ultimately have one foot in two kingdoms. Either you are in the kingdom of life, or you are in the kingdom of death; either you are a slave to righteousness, or a slave to sin; either you are receiving the gift of God, or receiving the pay envelope of death.

Now all of this is pretty shocking when it is put as bluntly as this. We may respond that Paul can't really mean these things because they are impossible. My only plea to the reader here is to look at the text as it stands and see if what I am saying is not what the text says. I believe it is.

Furthermore, all of this is completely consistent with the Old Testament. When God delivered his people from Egypt, there was nothing they could do to save themselves. If God did not deliver them, they would spend their lives in slavery. But after he had delivered them, he brought them to the foot of Sinai. There he asked of them absolute allegiance that would express itself in total obedience. And failure to render that obedience was, upon their own words, to result in death. Why did God require such things? Because he intended to take up residence among them. This is his goal for his people. They inherit the land, but *they* are the Lord's inheritance. And God cannot live in a defiled Temple. The covenant points to God's desire that his people shall be clean, not merely as a judicial fiction but as a matter of fact.

Neither Knowledge nor Effort Can Prevent Sin

So what is the next step in Paul's argument? It grows out of the imaginary hearer's response to the arguments of chapter 6. We can imagine that response going something like this: "Oh, now I understand, Paul. We were brought into a relationship with God by grace through faith, but to remain in that relationship we must live a holy life, and we do that by keeping the law. Right?" Paul answers,

"Wrong! You cannot keep the law. If you attempt to do that, the law will only damn you."

This is of course the same problem into which the Galatians fell. They came to believe that although we are saved by grace, we must afterwards work out that salvation by rigorous obedience. Paul's response there is to argue that the Christian life is never one in which our human effort secures the relationship. There, as in Romans, he uses the image of slavery. But in Galatians he says that to try to work out one's salvation by careful obedience to the law is to fall back into the slavery from which Christ delivered us. No, the Christian life is one of grace through faith operating from end to end.

Here Paul approaches the question from a slightly different angle. He asks, "Will rigorous obedience to the law produce the life in which sin has no dominion that I called for in chapter six?" And the answer is "No, for two reasons." The first reason is given in chapter 7, verses 1-6. He says that we are in a new era since the coming of Christ. The previous husband is dead, and we have married a new husband, so we are living under his aegis, and not that of the former husband. In fact, he says, the Law was not able to produce the righteousness that it demanded. Thus, all it could do was to condemn us. Why would we want to go back to a husband like that, he asks?

This leads to the main thought of the chapter, which is found in verses 8-25, and is a personal testimony of Paul. In answer to the suggestion that we are saved by grace, but continue the relationship by human effort, he says, "Oh no, that won't work! I know, I have been there. If you try to use the law to save yourself, either before or after accepting Christ, you doom yourself to endless frustration." This is why Paul uses the first person throughout these verses. He is not speaking of his present experience, and he is certainly not speaking of the "normal" Christian experience. To read the chapter in that way is to reduce chapter 6 to so much meaningless rhetoric, and it destroys the logic of chapter 8. Rather, when we read it in the way I am proposing here, the argument flows straight from chapter 6 to chapter 8 in clear logical progression. It is precisely because of Paul's own Jewish experience of trying to please God in his own strength and the frustration that it produced that he speaks with such energy and vividness here. To suggest that Christians cannot expect any more of Christ's reality in their lives than that which we find in Romans chapter 7 is a travesty.[25]

Paul is showing out of his own experience that the law is incapable of producing the righteousness that he called for in chapter 6. The law was not given as a ladder upon which people could climb into the presence of God. What was the law given for, then? It was given to show how holy God is, and how sinful we humans are. Here Paul is directly echoing the points made in the first part of this book on the Old Testament. But this echoing goes farther. Why is the law unable to make us righteous? Because of the human problem that the law exists to expose. What is that problem? Paul identifies it using the Greek word for "flesh." The New International Version, recognizing the problems created by this use of a physical term for a spiritual problem, usually translates the word with "the sinful nature." But this obscures as much as it illuminates, because of the complex connotations of the term in different contexts.

In general, the New Testament uses "flesh" in four different ways. It can use it in an entirely physical sense, and when used in this way it has a good connotation (in contrast to the way the Greeks thought of the flesh). So when Paul says Christ came in the "flesh" (Col. 1:21-22), he is saying that was a good thing. The second way the text uses flesh is to speak of those desires which are related to bodily needs, thus the desires for sleep, food, water, sex, etc. (Eph. 2:3). These can be good

---

[25]There is considerable difference of opinion among commentators as to whether 7:13-25 refers to Paul's pre-conversion or post-conversion experience. A. Nygren (*Commentary on Romans*, tr. C. Rasmussen, London: SCM, 1952), himself an advocate of the post-conversion position, charts the history of interpretation thus (pp. 284-286): the majority of Church Fathers held the pre-conversion stance; this changed with Augustine and continued through the Reformers; the Pietists reverted to the position of the Fathers, and there is no unanimity at present. Some recent advocates of the pre-conversion position (in one form or another) are: R. Bultmann, *Romer 7 und die Anthropologie des Paulus*, 1932; C. H. Dodd, *The Epistle of Paul to the Romans*, Moffat New Testament Commentaries, London: Hodder and Stoughton, 1932; D. Moo, *Romans 1-8*, Wycliffe Exegetical Commentary, ed. K. Barker, Chicago: Moody, 1991.

or bad depending on the degree to which one's life is dominated by them. If they are under control, they are essentially good. The remaining two uses speak of attitudes, and both are bad. In the first case, the "flesh" refers to that attitude which says that all there is to life is the satisfaction of bodily desire, and the acquisition of physical possessions (1 John 2:16). In other words, it is the attitude that dominates much of the modern media culture. The final use of "flesh" speaks of that attitude which makes human ability paramount. Thus, it refers to human pride and self-will (1 Cor. 1:26). It is these last two uses which the NIV usually translates with "the sinful nature."

This New Testament concept of "the flesh" is similar to the Old Testament ideas of the "spirit of prostitution" or the "evil imagination." It is that in us which predisposes us to want our way instead of God's way. It is that which insists upon determining all matters of right and wrong for itself, and since it is in rebellion against God, it inevitably calls evil, good and good, evil. When it concludes that living in accordance with God's standards is in its best interests, it will do so, but not for love of God. Thus, it will never be able to do God's will, always falling short of the best, because doing God's will first of all requires surrendering my own will, something that is impossible for "the flesh." The flesh is that in a child or in an adult which says, "I'll do it by myself, and I'll do it my own way."

So, verses 14-18 read as follows:

> We know that the law is spiritual; but I am unspiritual (fleshly), sold as a slave to sin. I do not understand what I do. For what I want to do I do not do, but what I hate I do. And if I do what I do not want to do, I agree that the law is good. As it is, it is no longer I myself who do it, but it is sin living in me. I know that nothing good lives in me, that is, in my sinful nature (flesh). For I have the desire to do what is good, but I cannot carry it out.

Paul is making three points here. First of all, he is saying that it is no fault of the law that it cannot make me righteous. The law is good and spiritual. The problem is in me, in my "flesh." That is, as we saw above, there is a flaw in the human spirit, something that makes me prefer the tainted to the pure. This is the second point. The third is that the person who attempts to keep the law in their "flesh" will be involved in a hopeless contradiction. They will be seeking to do something spiritual with an instrument that is profoundly opposed to the spiritual values being espoused. The "flesh" wants to please itself, to gain power for itself, and to assert its own will. All of these are profoundly opposed by the law. So I will choose to do something and discover myself doing the very opposite.

Again, I emphasize that Paul is not speaking about normal Christian experience here. He said very clearly that you cannot be a slave to sin and a slave to Christ at the same time (6:15-18) and here he says that the person who tries to keep the law in their own strength will be "sold as a slave to sin." Paul is speaking out of his experience as a Jew to caution the person who thinks that they can live a holy life in their own strength. He says our "flesh" will frustrate us at every point if we ever try to do that. There is a "law of sin at work within my members" (v. 23) so that I am trapped in a "body of death" (v. 24). Here again he is directly echoing that frustration with which the Old Testament closed. The Jews affirmed that the Torah was good and should be obeyed, but they had found that "the imaginations of the thoughts of their hearts were wholly evil" (Gen. 6:5).

This then brings us to the third of Paul's dialogical questions. The first began chapter 6: since no righteousness of mine brought me to Christ, no righteousness is expected of me in the relationship with Christ. Paul answered that with a thundering "No." We have died to sin with Christ; how could we think that we could continue to live in sin? The second question is implied at the beginning of chapter 7: "All right, I come into the relationship with Christ by faith, and I am expected to live a life of righteousness. So do I do that by my own effort through obedience to the law? Again Paul answers with a strong "No." The law cannot make us righteous, because we are creatures of the "flesh," profoundly opposed to what the law stands for. All that our attempts to keep the law will do is to expose how thoroughly the "flesh" (the lust of the eyes, the lust of the flesh, and the pride of life) has us in its grip. The third question then grows out of the conflict between the answers to the first and the second. If to be a Christian is to live a life of righteousness like Christ's and yet I am unable to live such a life, what am I to do? The issue is well expressed in 7:24: "What a wretched man I am! Who will rescue me from this body of death?" Paul's imaginary hearer cries, "Paul, you have backed me into a corner where I cannot get out. You say I must be righteous, but that I cannot be. You say I must be a slave of Christ, but that I am a slave to sin. Help!"

If You Live by the Spirit
You Will Not Do the Works of the Flesh

Chapter 8 is Paul's solution to this apparently hopeless contradiction. That it is such is widely recognized, but the way it is often interpreted unfortunately misses the central point of the chapter almost completely, because of the previous misreading of chapter 7. What the chapter says in a nutshell is this: the way to defeat sin in our lives is to allow the Spirit of Christ to live his life through us. In this way the "flesh" will not be allowed to rule us, and we will not continue in sin. This is of course exactly what the Old Testament promises of the coming of the Spirit envisioned. We would be enabled to fulfill the just requirements of the covenant by means of God's Spirit taking up residence in us after we had been cleansed from the sins of the past.

Now let's look at the chapter in more detail. Perhaps the most striking feature of the chapter is that the word "spirit" occurs no less than 15 times in the first 16 verses, and a further five times in verses 23-27! And this after the word has only appeared four times in the entire previous seven chapters! It is also significant that fully 18 of these 20 references are to God's Spirit, the Holy Spirit. Surely Paul is attempting to make a point here! That point is that the Christian life is not one of striving to be holy in our own strength (our "flesh"), but one which is lived out through the energy of God's own Spirit.

Notice the first four verses:

> Therefore, there is now no condemnation for those who are in Christ Jesus, because through Christ Jesus the law of the Spirit of life set me free from the law of sin and death. For what the law

was powerless to do in that it was weakened by the [flesh], God did by sending his own Son in the likeness of sinful man to be a sin offering. And so he condemned sin in sinful man, in order that the righteous requirements of the law might be fully met in us, who do not live according to the [flesh] but according to the Spirit.

Many persons who interpret chapter 7 to mean that Christians cannot help but sin, read these verses as an approval of this point of view. They read these verses as saying that because of Christ's death we are not condemned even though we continue to be slaves to the law of sin (7:25). Thus, the passage would be saying that since Christ has died as a sin offering for us, God looks upon us as having fulfilled the law even though we do not do so.

But that is clearly not what the passage is saying. Paul does not say that Christ has set us free from the *curse* of the law of sin and death, but that he has set us free from the *law* of sin and death *itself*. At the end of chapter 7 Paul testifies that when he attempted to obey God in his own strength (his flesh) he found himself "a slave to the law of sin." But now through Christ he says he is *not* a slave to that law any longer. Chapter 7 does not describe the normal Christian life in Paul's mind. Chapter 8 describes what that life is intended to be. Further confirmation of this point appears in the final sentence in the passage. Why did Christ make an offering of himself? In order to "condemn sin" in us so "that the righteous requirements of the law might be fully met in us." How does he do that ? Merely judicially? Are we legally forgiven although we continue to do that which caused us to be condemned in the first place? Not at all. We were unable to live the kinds of righteous lives which the covenant requires because of the self-centeredness which Paul calls "the flesh." And because of that sinfulness, God's Holy Spirit could not live in us to enable us to do so. Thus, the deadly downward spiral which Paul described in chapter 7.

So what has Christ done? He has made himself a sin offering so that we could be cleansed through the forgiveness of our sins, thus making it possible for the Holy Spirit to take up residence in us and enable us to live God's holy life. In other words, this is exactly what was envisioned by Ezekiel in chapter 36 as discussed above. Christ has not come to free us from any necessary obedience to God. Far from it! He has come to make it possible for us to obey him, thus finding our true selves in living out the Divine character we were made for. That this is Paul's point is confirmed by the final clause of the sentence. The righteous requirements of the law will be lived out if we "do not live according to the flesh but according to the Spirit." The apostle is not saying that we can live according to the flesh [as we must, according to some interpreters] and yet experience forgiveness through Christ. He is saying that through Christ it is now possible not to live by the flesh with its inevitable result of failure and increasing bondage, but according to the Holy Spirit's life and power.

If any question remained that this was Paul's point, the uncertainty must certainly be put to rest by the next two paragraphs, verses 5-11:

> Those who live according to the [flesh] have their minds set on what [the flesh] desires; but those who live in accordance with the Spirit have their minds set on what the Spirit desires. The [fleshly] mind is death, but the mind controlled by the Spirit is life and peace; because the [fleshly] mind is hostile to God. It does not submit to God's law, nor can it do so. Those controlled by the [flesh] cannot please God.

> You, however, are controlled not by the [flesh] but by the Spirit, if the Spirit of God lives in you. And if anyone does not have the Spirit of Christ, he does not belong to Christ. But if Christ is in you, your body [different word from "flesh"] is dead because of sin, yet your spirit is alive because of righteousness. And if the Spirit of him who raised Jesus from the dead is living in you, he who raised Christ from the dead will also give life to your mortal bodies through his Spirit, who lives in you.

From these words we can see very clearly that Paul does not by any means envision the conflicted life described in Romans 7 as normal. In fact, he shows here that it is impossible for a Christian to live in such a condition. The persons who attempt to live God's life in their own strength and in order to please themselves—that is, in the flesh—are doing so with an attitude that is "hostile" to God. It is so because God calls us to surrender our own efforts and goals to him. Not to do so is to persist in our own pride and self-serving—the way of death. Those who attempt to serve God in that way can never please him.

But the Christian is not controlled by the flesh (v. 9)! This verse alone should rule out any thought that 7:14-25 is describing a normal Christian. Paul's reasoning is crystal clear, even though he has put it in reverse order. If we put it in normal order, it is even clearer: (1)If you belong to Christ you have the Spirit of Christ; (2) If the Spirit of God lives in you, you cannot be controlled by the flesh. So Paul is making it perfectly clear that what was being talked about in chapter 7 is the impossibility of fulfilling the command of chapter 6 in ones own strength—the flesh. Such an attempt will only land you in a kind of slavery which is absolutely contrary to the freedom in obedience which is what the Christian life is about. But Jesus has made it possible for the Old Testament promises of the Holy Spirit to be fulfilled. He is the one who will make it possible for us to live out God's covenant life, which is what chapter 6 is talking about.

In verses 10 and 11 Paul engages in a lovely bit of word-play which underlines his point. He says that because all humans have chosen to serve the "flesh," our "bodies" have become subject to death. And, as he has already said, if we persist in serving the "flesh" our spirits will die forever with our bodies. But if we have become Christians, then even though our bodies will die, our spirits will not die with them. In fact, because we have chosen to serve the Spirit, our bodies will be restored to life with our spirits! Serve the flesh with our spirits, and our dead bodies will drag our spirits down to eternal death; serve the Spirit and deny the flesh, and our resurrected spirits will share that resurrection life with our bodies.

In verses 12-16, Paul continues this theme, bringing this part of his argument to a climax with the insistence that we are not slaves of a law we can never keep, but sons of God, heirs of the kingdom.

> Therefore, brothers, we have an obligation—but it is not to the [flesh], to live according to it. For if you live according to the [flesh], you will die; but if by the Spirit you put to death the misdeeds of the body, you will live, because those who are led by

the Spirit of God are sons of God. For you did not receive a spirit
that makes you a slave again to fear, but you received the Spirit
of sonship. And by him we cry, "*Abba*, Father." The Spirit
himself testifies with our spirit that we are God's children.

Again, the point here is unmistakable. As Christians, we must live the
life of the Spirit. There is no other way. We cannot have one foot in the
kingdom of sin, and one in the kingdom of life. We *must* live in the
Spirit. To do anything else would be to deny our true parentage. We
must die to the life of the flesh and we must put to death all that
springs from that life. But these "musts" mask a much deeper truth.
It is not so much that we "must" do these things as that we "may"! To
attempt to live the life of God in our own strength is indeed to fall into
a life of slavery—dual slavery: slavery to the higher life we know we
ought to live but cannot, and slavery to a lower life which we hate but
cannot avoid. In place of that slavery Paul shows us a picture of
family. We *are* God's children, through the blessed Spirit whom the
Son has made available, and all we need to do is to cooperate in the life
that is naturally ours as children of the Father. Yes, because of the flaw
in the human spirit, which Paul lumps together in the word "flesh," the
Old Covenant was weak. It could not give us the Father's life that it
called us to share. But Christ has done what the Old Covenant could
not. Through his perfect sacrifice he has made Jeremiah's dream
possible: now by the power of the Holy Spirit God's covenant is
written on our hearts. Now we are happy to name ourselves as the
sons and daughters of God. Now God's goal from the beginning can
be realized. Now he can not only live his life among us, but, best of all,
in us, in Temples which are clean and in which every shining surface
is a mirror of his own face.

Paul has one more point to make in this chapter before he launches
into a lyrical conclusion. It is found in verses 17-30. Here Paul speaks
of the necessity of perseverance. We are mistaken if we think that the
life of a child of heaven's king in this world is one of unrelieved
pleasure and comfort. To be sure, glory lies at the end of the way
(vv. 17-18, 30). But the present creation is marred, and like us, it
groans for its final redemption (19-23). The evidence of the Spirit

within us encourages us to hope, but it is hope and not yet possession (23-25). Yet while we wait, groaning for our final redemption, the Spirit is our Intercessor, groaning with us and for us until that final day (26-30).

This brings us to the final paragraph in the chapter (vv. 31-39), in which Paul waxes lyrical over the marvelous conclusion that the line of reasoning in the previous chapters inevitably reaches. If the only Judge of the universe has in fact become our Advocate, then there is no possible case against us! If the One whom we have offended is now our Intercessor, then it is possible to live his life and fulfill his calling. We are no longer slaves to what we hate, but sons and daughters who are "more than conquerors." Nothing can keep us from experiencing the Divine love that the covenant first set before the eyes of the Hebrew people standing in awe at the foot of Sinai.

This wonderful conclusion is not merely to chapter 8, as some think it. These persons see these verses as hymning the good news that although we are slaves to sin in our flesh, God willfully blinds himself to that fact for Christ's sake and loves us as though we did not sin. As I have shown, this is not what chapter 8 teaches at all. Chapter 8 is showing us that we are *not* slaves to sin because of the Spirit who dwells within us as Christians. Because of this Spirit we can conquer the flesh and are enabled to keep the covenant, as chapter 6 (and indeed the entire Scripture) commands us. So this conclusion is to the entire train of thought which began in 1:16. Chapters 1-3 show that we are separated from the love of God because of our sin. Then chapters 4 and 5 tell us that we can become righteous and be brought into fellowship with God through an act of faith. But chapter 6 shows us that although it was faith that reconciled us to God, that does not relieve us of the necessity for righteous living. But we should not fall back into thinking that we can somehow produce that righteousness in our own strength. That way will lead to disaster, as chapter 7 shows. No, as chapter 8 demonstrates, just as reconciliation is the result of grace operating through faith, so is righteousness. As we accept our reconciliation by faith, so we also live out the new life of the Spirit by faith, with the result that what the law could never do, the Holy Spirit does do in us, and we are reshaped into the likeness of our Father. That—all that—is the cause for Paul's joy in 8:31-39. No longer are we rebels or sullen slaves; no, we are the children of God, conquerors of what is without, and even more, what is within. What indeed, can separate us from the love of God in Christ Jesus our Lord?

9

The Ministry of Jesus
and the Life of Holiness

In the previous chapter I attempted to show from chapters 6-8 of Romans that the same pattern which we saw in the Old Testament is present in the New. In the Old Testament the required response to gracious salvation was righteous living. God's deliverance of his people was not an end in itself. Rather, he delivered them in order that he might have fellowship with them. But such fellowship was impossible unless the people agreed to an exclusive relationship with him in which they agreed to live lives like his, that is, holy lives. This is exactly the pattern Paul follows in Romans 6. Having shown how deliverance from the condemnation of sin is possible through faith in Christ, he shows that fellowship with this saving Christ is impossible unless we renounce sin in all its ramifications.

But in the Old Testament, the people's attempts to keep their covenant were met with an almost mystifying inability to do so. The harder they attempted to do what both they and God wanted, the more marked became their failures. In the end they had to believe that there was in them a positive bent away from whatever was good, and right, and pure, and toward whatever was evil, perverse, and deceitful. Paul discusses this in Romans 7 as he counsels his readers not to misunderstand him by thinking that they can fulfill the commands of chapter 6 in their own strength, or "flesh." Whatever we do in our own strength will be tainted by that bent away from God, and we will never be able to please him in that way.

So what did the Old Testament believers recognize was the cure for their problem? How were they to be able to keep the covenant and live in the presence of God, as they wished to do and as they knew was the very best thing for them? The answer would be the coming of God's Holy Spirit to take up residence in them, giving them the power to live the life of God in a way which the bent human spirit can never do.

Again, Paul is in perfect agreement with this point of view. How shall we keep the commandments of God's covenant? How shall we live the holy life that is necessary if we are to enjoy God's fellowship? Through the Holy Spirit! The same Spirit through whom the Father raised his Son has been made available to us who died with Christ on the Cross. Through his energy flowing through us we can renounce the flesh and all its works. Our divided hearts can be made one, and we can live holy lives for God's sake.

We may see this same point being emphasized in Jesus' ministry. We have already noted that John expected the chief result of Jesus' ministry was to make the Spirit available to his people. When we look at what is recorded of Jesus' preaching we do not hear him saying a great deal about the Holy Spirit, although what he does say is very significant as we will see before the end of this chapter. What we do hear a great deal of is the Kingdom of God, or the Kingdom of Heaven. What we do not hear much about is substitutionary atonement procuring salvation so that persons can go to heaven after death. This is not to say there is none of such teaching present in Jesus' ministry (see for instance John 3:1-21, or Matt. 26:26-29). Nor am I suggesting that Paul has introduced something alien to the thought of Jesus when he makes Jesus' atoning death so central to the Christian message. What I am saying is that Jesus' ultimate concern was, like Paul's, not with whether people got *into* the kingdom, but that having entered the kingdom they should be transformed and live their lives not for themselves but for the King and for others.

In passage after passage we find Jesus talking about whether people have discovered how to be free of their own selfish interests in order to live freely for God. So he calls them to generosity, to faithfulness, to forgiveness, to the kind of changed living which demonstrates the reality of repentance. What is the sin for which he so bitterly castigates the Pharisees? They are trying to keep the commandments of God in their own strength so that they can make themselves acceptable to God. This is a denial of that kind of changed heart that was so central to Jesus' concerns. He calls for a self-forgetfulness that puts the needs of others before our own, that makes us love God for himself and not for what we can get out of it. This is kingdom living, but by the same token, it could also be called covenant living. It is what Jesus means when he says he has come to fulfill the law. Yes, God wants our obedience, but much more than that he wants us. This is what Jesus is trying to communicate. But that is not a new thought. Already in Psalm 51 David recognizes it when he says that the sacrifice God wants is a "crushed heart." Moses recognizes it when he says that God wants a circumcised heart (Deut. 10:16). And Jeremiah and Ezekiel recognized it when they predicted that the day would come when God would remove hearts of stone and write his law on hearts that were soft and tender.

What I am saying here is that Jesus' concern is not fundamentally different than that of the Old Testament. Salvation for Jesus did not involve forgiveness so that people could continue to live lives that were a disgrace but now with a good conscience. Salvation for him was kingdom living and kingdom living required making the King the exclusive ruler of your heart and then living a life which was in complete keeping with the standards of that kingdom. Tragically, Jesus' words have come to be treated as a lovely, but utterly unrealistic, ideal; one which we should all strive for, but which no one but the odd saint or two could ever hope to reach.

Why has this happened? It has happened to a large extent because we have divorced Jesus' ministry from what both he and John the Baptist thought was the culmination of his ministry: Pentecost. Instead of seeing Pentecost as the culmination of Jesus' ministry we have tended to treat it as one of the events which happened after Jesus' ascension. Perhaps it was the most important of these events, but it was just one of several. It is particularly John's gospel which makes the fallacy of this approach clear. In what is known as the Last Supper Discourse, Jesus sought to prepare his disciples for what lay ahead for them. Intrinsic to all that he said was his promise to send the Holy Spirit to them. How were they to live out the stupendous things that he had taught? How were they to live out the kingdom principles that he had laid down? Their failures were displayed on every hand. They clearly had no understanding of the significance of the Cross for kingdom living. Like the children of Israel, they were willing to obey, but they seemed incapable of it. They thought only of themselves and their prerogatives. All of the stories of the disciples which we find in the Gospels after the confession of Peter are stories of failure. Surely if the witness of the kingdom depends on these people after Jesus' ascension, the cause is a lost one.

But the cause was not lost. As a result of the disciples' witness the world was turned upside down. What happened? What happened is that the thing Jesus was seeking to prepare the disciples for, and the thing that he commanded them to wait for before attempting any ministry, came to pass. The day of Pentecost came and all the hope of the ages came to realization—the promised Holy Spirit came. He was the one for whom the Old Testament prophets had hoped. He was the One who made the Messiah's kingdom possible. In him Moses' command, echoed across so many years, became a possibility: "You shall love the LORD your God with all your heart and with all your soul and with all your strength" (Deut. 6:5).

What did Jesus expect that the Holy Spirit would do to make the realization of his kingdom possible? Let's look at his words in John. The key passages in the Last Supper Discourse are 14:15-27 and 16:5-16. They are too long to quote in their entirety here, but we will quote shorter sections as we come to them.

The way in which Jesus opens the discussion in chapter 14 is very significant. He says, "If you love me, you will obey what I command. And I will ask the Father, and he will give you another Counselor to be with you forever—the Spirit of Truth" (15-17a). The significance of the statement is that it precisely mirrors the pattern of the Old Testament: obedience is an expression of love that is the response to God's prior grace. But Jesus immediately assumes what it took Old Testament believers nearly a millennium to discover: that obedience is only possible if God himself empowers us to do so through his Spirit. This is of course the very same point that we saw Paul making in the first eight chapters of Romans. Why is the Holy Spirit given? To enable us to obey our Savior.

If there were any doubt about this point, it should be dispelled by Jesus' reiteration of it in verse 21: "Whoever has my commands and obeys them, he is the one who loves me. He who loves me will be loved by my Father, and I too will love him and show myself to him." In verses 17b-20 Jesus has made the point that the Spirit will be in them and that will mean Jesus himself is in them, for although he will shortly leave them, he will also shortly return to them, making possible an incredible union between him and them and the Father. From this point it would have been very easy for Jesus to wax lyrical about mystical union with the Divine, etc. But that is just what he does not do. Instead, he returns to the beginning point of his teaching. The evidence of the mystical love union will be obedience! How very mundane. And yet how central to everything which the Bible teaches us. What does it mean to be holy? To somehow partake of the divine essence? Not at all. To be holy is to obey the commands of God for love's sake. And this is what the Holy Spirit, the Spirit of Jesus, has come to enable us to do. In this regard it is important to take note of the description of the Spirit which Jesus reverts to several times: the Spirit of Truth (14:17; 15:26; 16:13). As we saw in our study of the Old Testament, one of the characteristics of God that marked him as holy was his truth. This is not so much the idea that what is said by God is true, although that is certainly a valid implication. Rather, it is that God is absolutely faithful and utterly reliable. He is true, unlike the gods who lie and deceive both their worshippers and one another as they pursue their own ravenous self-interest. This God is One, both in his essence and in his character. Thus, it can hardly be incidental that

Jesus identifies the Holy Spirit as "the Spirit of Truth." God has called us to share his character and, perhaps more than anything else, that means we are called to be true—both to him and to one another. But how shall we, so deeply corrupt and deceitful, ever aspire to truth like his? To his glory, it is possible as the Spirit of Truth takes up his residence in us.

Judas (Thaddeus) was interested in the physical question of why Jesus could be seen by the disciples but not by the world (v. 22). But Jesus refused to be sidetracked by the question and went right on as if he had not been interrupted, hammering home the inseparable connection between love and obedience (vv. 23-24). Not to obey is not to love, but to love is to obey. And the person who loves by obeying will experience the presence of the Father and the Son taking up their residence in him. This entire thing is the work of the Spirit. He inspires our love for Christ as well as the ensuing desire to obey him. And he is the one who empowers us for that obedience through the indwelling presence of the Father and the Son.

In chapter 16 we see Jesus making a similar point. Jesus says that it is a good thing he is going away. How could that possibly be? How could Jesus' departure be a good thing? Because that is the only way the "One who Comes Alongside"—the One who encourages, strengthens, and defends—can come to us. Why is that a good thing? Because Jesus in his physical body can only be in one place at one time. Furthermore, in that state he can only be *with* his disciples, not *in* them. But the Holy Spirit, whom Jesus makes clear is himself in another form, can be with and in all of us simultaneously. "Christ in you," Paul's joyous promise (Col. 1:27), is made possible by the Holy Spirit. And what will he do in us? "When he comes, he will convict the world of guilt in regard to sin and righteousness and judgment" (16:8). That is, the function of the Holy Spirit will be directly and specifically related to the issues of obedience. The following words are somewhat enigmatic:

> in regard to sin, because men do not believe in me; in regard to righteousness, because I am going to the Father, where you can

see me no longer; and in regard to judgment, because the Prince
of this world now stands condemned. (16:9-11)

A number of different interpretations of this passage have been put
forward over the years, but I would like to suggest that the most
natural one is this: the Holy Spirit will enable Jesus' disciples to live
lives of such a sterling quality that men and women will be convinced
that it is a sin not to believe in Jesus. Furthermore, although Jesus is
no longer on the earth, they will see the righteousness of Jesus in the
disciples and will be convicted of their own lack of righteousness.
Finally, this remarkable quality of life in the disciples, one of love and
faithfulness and truth, will be powerful evidence that the Prince of the
World has been defeated and that therefore he and all who follow him
are facing judgment.

This understanding is supported by the content of chapter 15.
There Jesus talked about the nature of his living in his disciples
through the Spirit by using the image of a vine and its branches. The
Spirit does not live in us as a device we can use to achieve our own
goals. More correctly we live in him and function as extensions of him
for the achievement of his goals. Again in verses 9-17 Jesus emphasizes
the inseparable connection between love and obedience, saying that
obedience is love and love is obedience. But this obedience is not
that of slavery. It is the obedience born of friendship. We love him and
want to walk with him as his friends; therefore we want to do whatever
it is that he wants.

In 15:18-25 Jesus tells the disciples that they will be hated by the
world just as he was. The world hates Jesus for two reasons: 1) He is
manifestly not a part of this world system (19, 21); 2) He has spoken
words and performed miracles which call the world to decide for
him and against themselves, and the people of the world are unwilling
to do so (22-25).

Then in verses 26-27 Jesus states: "When the Counselor comes,
whom I will send to you from the Father, the Spirit of Truth who goes
out from the Father, he will testify about me; but you also must testify,
for you have been with me from the beginning."

This statement is important in the way it relates both to what precedes it and what follows it. Jesus is saying that the Holy Spirit will continue what Jesus had done in the world, demonstrating his holiness and the world's sinfulness. But he also says that the Spirit will do this through the witness of the disciples. Thus we are prepared for the words of 16:5-11. The particular obedience that love demands will be made possible by the Spirit of Christ in the disciples. The result will be that the world will continue to see the evidence that it is a sin not to believe in Christ, that righteous living is a real possibility, and that the Prince of this world has been defeated. This is what Jesus Christ says will be made possible by his "going away" (16:7). Of course, this is a very minimalist way of describing the relationship between the ministries of the Son and the Spirit. In fact, the ministry of the Spirit is nothing other than a continuation of the ministry of the Son on a worldwide plane, as 16:12-16 makes clear. As has been said before, the ministry of Jesus did not come to its completion with his atoning death. In a real sense, his temporal ministry *began* with the Cross, reached its midpoint in his resurrection and ascension, and came to its culmination in his return through the Holy Spirit. To be sure, his ministry continues and will only be complete in his final return in glory. But these three stages—death, resurrection, and Pentecost—capture what he came to do in his incarnation.

We have seen in this chapter how Jesus' understanding of his work, especially in relation to the coming of the Holy Spirit, is entirely consistent with Paul's understanding. Persons are called to enter into the Kingdom of God through repentance and faith, there to become not the slaves of the King, but his friends. The love that such grace would certainly invoke is to be expressed through obedience to the King's commands. But this obedience presupposes a unique identification of the kingdom people with the King in which there is an actual spiritual union between the two. The agent of this union is the Spirit of Truth, who is in fact Jesus in his ascended state. The fundamental consonance of this view with that of the Old Testament must be quite plain to those readers who have followed the argument of this book thus far.

But what does all this imply for the life of the average Christian? Surely it implies that Christ (and Paul) expect that the average Christian will live a life in which glad obedience to the commands of God is their normal practice. That is, they will be a holy people. It implies that there is no place for sin in their lives. It implies that they do not expect to sin, but expect to live the life of Christ day after day by the power of the Spirit. It implies that the world will be convicted of its own sinfulness and of its lost condition by a kind of Christian living which is a continual witness to the transforming power of Christ. But is this really possible? Is it really possible to live above sin? And does the New Testament really expect this? The answer to these questions is "Yes," and that will be the subject of the next chapter.

10

New Testament Expectations of Christian Life

In chapter 4 of part I we asked whether the Old Testament writers actually believed that it was possible to fulfill the stipulations of the covenant, and we looked at two concepts which showed that they did indeed believe such a thing. They were words that the Authorized Version often translated with the English word "perfect." One of these words had to do with living a life that was unblemished in God's sight. The other had to do with having motivations and desires that were wholly dedicated to God, and a will which was wholly his. The New Testament shows the same phenomena, particularly in the case of the first concept. There is clear evidence that the New Testament writers are familiar with the Old Testament concept and are carrying it over into the New Testament context. In this chapter we will look at that evidence first and then we will look at other cases where it is apparent that the New Testament writers thought a life which was marked by complete obedience to God was not merely possible but was the norm.

The Hebrew word used to describe a "perfect" sacrificial animal, one with no blemishes, is *tamim*. This Hebrew word is normally translated with various forms of one of two Greek words in the Septuagint, the ancient Greek version of the Old Testament. Those words are *teleios*, "complete, finished, perfect," and *amemphomai*, "without blame, blameless, guiltless." When we look at the way those two words are used in their various forms in the New Testament, it becomes clear that the New Testament writers are using the words just as the Greek translators of the Old Testament did. That is, they believe that it is not merely possible to live a life that is wholly dedicated to God and is thus blameless in his sight, it is expected.

The basic idea of *teleios* is wholeness, or completeness. Thus, it may refer to adulthood, as in 1 Corinthians 14:20, "Brothers, stop thinking like children. In regard to evil be infants, but in your thinking be *adults*." In the same way, it may be translated as "mature," as in Hebrews 5:13-14, "Anyone who lives on milk, being still an infant, is not acquainted with the teaching about righteousness. But solid food is for the *mature*, who by constant use have trained themselves to distinguish good from evil." But this latter reference shows us that the word has more in mind than what is usually connoted by the English word "mature." In English "mature" usually means full-grown, and may also connote having balanced judgment. *Teleios* goes beyond this. It connotes having arrived at all that can be expected of something or someone. So in the case of a sacrificial animal, if some normal part is missing or deformed, that animal is not complete as we have a right to expect it to be. Thus, an infant is an incomplete human. It may be a perfect baby, but it is not yet a perfect human. Something is missing from them, whether physically, mentally, or emotionally. They are not all that they can be expected to be. In Hebrews the writer is suggesting that a Christian can reach a state of completeness with regard to distinguishing right from wrong, whether in Christian doctrine, or in Christian behavior.

Paul shares the same thought when he says in Ephesians 4:13 "until we reach unity in the faith and in the knowledge of the Son of God and become *mature*, attaining to the whole measure of the fullness of Christ." Paul is not speaking merely about being a Christian who has good judgment and wisdom. No, he is speaking about someone who is all that could be expected of a Christian, someone who is filled with Christ to the highest degree that could be expected.

Interestingly, the New International Version, which as in the Old Testament, is much more leery of translating *teleios* with "perfect" than was the Authorized Version, is willing to translate it so in Colossians 1:28, where Paul is speaking of the same thing as in Ephesians 4. "We proclaim him, admonishing and teaching everyone with all wisdom, so that we may present every one *perfect* in Christ." This is a better translation than the one we find in James 1:4, "Perseverance must finish its work so that you may be *mature* and complete, not lacking anything." As the end of the sentence shows, the writer is not talking about our becoming "older" Christians, as "mature" connotes in English. He is talking about our becoming "perfect" Christians, that is, Christians whose life and behavior lacks nothing of that which could justly be expected of a follower of Christ.

When we recognize that *teleios* denotes completeness or wholeness, just as *tamim* does in the Old Testament, we are in a position to recognize its significance in such passages as Romans 12:2 which speaks of the "perfect," or complete, will of God. So also Hebrews 9:11 speaks of a "more perfect tabernacle that is not man-made." The earthly tabernacle was but a symbol of the spiritual truth that reached its perfection in the atonement and intercession of Christ. James speaks of God's giving good and *perfect* gifts (1:17), that is, gifts which are all that they should be, all that could be expected of them. Likewise, he describes God's plan for us as being "the *perfect* law of liberty." That is, God's plan is complete and without defect.

But *teleios* not only connotes wholeness and completeness. It also connotes being brought to the appropriate end. This is especially so when the word appears in the Greek perfect (completed) tense. So Luke 2:43 says, "After the feast was *over*," and Jesus speaks of "*reaching His goal*" (Luke, 13:32), or of "*finishing*" his work (John. 4:34; 5:36; 17:4). Paul uses the word in the same way in Acts 20:24 when he speaks about "*finishing* his course." Thus, to "perfect" something is to finish it, to bring it to completion, to cause it to reach that end for which it was created.

We have already noted above some instances where it is said that Christians can be made *teleios*, made whole, complete, without defect, brought to the desired end. Now I want to look at those and similar references in more detail. Do they really mean what they seem to be saying? Can Christians look into that perfect law of liberty and be made perfect as James says? We must begin with Jesus. In Matthew 5:48 he says in no uncertain terms, "Be *perfect*, therefore, as your heavenly Father is *perfect.*" There is no gainsaying these words. They are as stark and plain as the words of Leviticus, "You must be holy because I am holy." Furthermore, it is clear that this is no judicial perfection, but one which expresses itself in behavior. God's love toward people is not mixed, but perfect. Our love is to be of the same sort. Obviously, Jesus thinks this is possible or He would not have commanded it.[26]

This idea of perfect love is continued by Paul in 1 Corinthians 13:10 when he speaks of love as being the "perfect" gift before which the "imperfect" gifts of tongues and prophecy disappear. He says that to love is to think like an adult and no longer as a child.

The thought is carried on in 1 John where the apostle says,

> And so we know and rely on the love God has for us. God is love. Whoever lives in love lives in God, and God in him. Love is made complete among us so that we will have confidence on the day of judgment, because in this world we are like him. There is no fear in love. But perfect love drives out fear, because fear has to do with punishment. The man who fears is not made perfect in love. (4:16-18)

What is John talking about here? He is saying that it is possible for a Christian to love God and others completely, in a finished manner. He is saying that it is possible for Christians to experience a love which is, from God's point of view, without defect. He is saying that it is possible for a Christian to experience an unreserved love for God and a self-forgetful love for others. In other words he is saying that

---

[26]This verse shows that "maturity" in the limited modern sense is an inadequate translation for *teleios*. Imagine translating the verse "You must be mature as God is mature"!

what Jesus commanded is not merely an ideal, and not even a possibility, but is an expectation.

This same thought is confirmed in Paul and the other apostles. What is the goal of Paul's ministry, to get people to heaven? Well, it is certainly true that he wants to give them a certainty of their acceptance in the beloved, and he clearly wants to give them a living hope. These should not be overlooked or downplayed. But neither should we overlook or downplay an even more prominent goal. We have already noticed one expression of this in Colossians 1:28 and Ephesians 4:13. Paul wants to bring Christians to the point where they are all that could possibly be expected of them: perfect. And what is a "perfect" Christian? As with the sacrificial animals in the Old Testament, they are without defect. This does not mean that only "show animals" were acceptable as sacrifices. It simply meant that no one could look at the animal and say, "Look here, one leg is shorter than the others!" Neither could they say, "This animal has parasites." Neither could they say, "This animal is sick." No one could point out any defects in the animal. They might not win a prize in a show, but they were perfect. That is what Paul wanted for all his converts. He wanted the world to look at them and see nothing but Christlikeness. He did not want people to see Christians who were obviously lacking some aspect of the fullness of Christ. And he clearly believed that such a thing was not merely desirable or possible. As with John, it was expected.

This concept is especially prominent in the book of Hebrews where the writer is concerned that his readers are in a state of arrested development and are not going on to "perfection" (NIV "maturity").[27] Clearly, a part of his readers' problem was that they were confused about the relation between Christ and the Old Covenant. So the writer shows that the Old Covenant could not achieve its goal; it could not make anyone "perfect" (7:19; 10:1). The provisions of that

---

[27]On the inadequacy of the translation "maturity" in this kind of context, note the inconsistency of the NIV translation. In 7:11 "perfection" is used without any clear difference in the contextual setting. Is "perfection" objectionable in 6:1 because of its suggestion of the possibility of arrival at some point? But that is just what *teleios* is meant to imply, as its use in 7:11 indicates.

covenant were inadequate because they could not "perfect" (NIV "clear") the consciences of the worshippers (9:9). The only way the Old Testament saints would attain their goal of perfection was by means of their fellowship with us in the New Covenant (11:40). Christ has by his one sacrifice "made perfect" forever those who are being made holy (10:14). In other words, Christ has done for us what the Law could not do, very much what Paul said in Romans 8. But as there, this is not some sort of judicial standing where we are given "perfect" status, while living lives which are quite unlike Christ's. Hebrews 10:19-39 describes a life-style where sin has no part. Yes, as in the Old Testament, if a person should sin unintentionally, the blood of Christ's sacrifice will continue to cleanse us. But if a person deliberately makes a place for sin in their lives, there is no sacrifice left for them. The similarities with Romans 6 are unmistakable.

The conclusion of the teaching on perfection in Hebrews appears in the final chapter in the hortatory prayer of verses 20-21:

> May the God of peace, who through the blood of the eternal covenant brought back from the dead our Lord Jesus, that great Shepherd of the sheep, make you perfect in every good work [NIV equip you with everything good] for doing his will, and may he work in us what is pleasing to him, through Jesus Christ, to whom be glory for ever and ever. Amen.

The word here translated "perfect" is *katartisai,* a synonym of *teleios,* which means to bring to a state of total repair or one of complete preparation (see Luke 4:21 and 6:40). Thus, although "prepare" or "equip" are not incorrect translations, they are not adequate expressions of the complete idea. It does not speak merely of equipping in some way, but in a final and complete way, that is, to equip perfectly. The confirmation that the meaning of "perfection" is correct is to be found in 1 Corinthians 1:10 and 2 Corinthians 13:9, and 11. In each of these places NIV is forced to read respectively "*perfectly* united," "our prayer is for your *perfection,*" and "Aim for *perfection.*" In each of these cases it is clear that it is not the preparation or the restoration itself which the word has in focus, but what the end of the preparation or restoration is. That end is completeness without defect. Thus the prayer of the writer to the Hebrews is that his readers will be perfectly fitted by the God of peace to do his will, exactly the same thing which Paul has in mind when he prays for the Corinthians' perfection and when he exhorts them to "aim for perfection." Peter shares the same sentiment when he prays "And the God of all grace, who called you to his eternal glory in Christ, after you have suffered a little while, will himself *perfect* [NIV restore] you and make you strong, firm, and steadfast."[28]

Before we leave the discussion of *teleios* and its related words, we need to consider the occurrences in Philippians 3:12 and 15, because they shed a very significant light upon what the New Testament is calling for when it speaks of a "perfect" life. Very frequently those who contest the point of view being presented here will point to 3:12 as proof that no degree of perfection is possible in this life. But when they do so, they fail to pay attention to 3:15, where the same word is used. Unfortunately, the modern translations contribute to the confusion by the inconsistent way in which they translate the two verses. In the New International Version they appear thus:

> Not that I have already obtained this, or have already been *made perfect*, but I press on to take hold of that for which Christ Jesus took hold of me. (3:12)

> All of us who are *mature* should take such a view of things. And if on some point you think differently, that too God will make clear to you. (3:15)

The point is that both of these terms are forms of *teleios* and there is no justification for not translating 3:15 with "perfect" just as in 3:12 (as AV did, in fact). Or if it is felt that "perfect" is too strong a translation in 3:15, then there is no basis for using it in 3:12. There too, one should read "already become mature." It is hard to find any other

---

[28]Note that although the only occurrence of words for perfection in Romans 12:1-3 is in regard to God's will, Paul is clearly talking about this same idea, bringing Christians to the place where they are able to offer themselves to God without reservation, and to do nothing more nor less than the perfect will of God.

explanation for the differing translations of the word in the modern translations than the unwillingness of the modern mind to believe that it is possible to live a life which is truly and completely all that Christ would want.

But if the word means the same thing in both verses, what is Paul talking about? In verse 12 he seems to say that he is not perfect, while in verse 15 he includes himself with those who are perfect! Surely the difference in translation is justified as an attempt to reconcile the apparent contradiction. In that case, why not use "mature" in verse 12 and "perfect" in verse 15? I fear it is because the modern mind has no difficulty claiming "maturity" (in the limited modern sense), but does have difficulty in claiming "perfection." But as we have shown above, *teleios* connotes full and complete possession of all the potential of the species being described. Thus, if one wished to use "maturity" to translate the Greek word, one should use something like "perfect maturity" to produce a fair translation.

No, arbitrarily changing how the word is translated will not solve the apparent contradiction in which Paul has involved himself. I want to deal with this important point in more detail in a later chapter, but I do not want to leave the reader hanging at this point. So let me simply say here that the way through the problem lies in realizing that Paul is speaking about two levels of perfection. There is an absolute perfection where no more growth in knowledge or in Christian experience is possible. This is what Paul is disclaiming in verse 12, and rightly so. On the other hand, he does claim to have reached one level of completeness that he rightly refuses to describe as anything other than "perfection" in verse 15. This condition is described in verses 13-14. Paul is completely surrendered to Christ and to the outworking of God's will in his life. He can never be more surrendered than he is at this moment and he can never be more committed to doing the will of God. In this sense Paul is more than willing to include himself among those who are without blemish in their relation to Christ. This does not mean that Paul's performance or his knowledge is necessarily unblemished. That is the area where he knows further growth is both possible and necessary. But at the level of his surrender and of his determination to do nothing other than the will of God, he is *tamim, teleios,* perfect.. This is reminiscent of what we saw of Asa in the Old Testament. His heart was "perfect" toward God, even though through an imperfect understanding he did not destroy the high places outside of Jerusalem where God was also worshipped.

The second Greek word that is used to translate the Hebrew *tamim* functions very similarly to *teleios*. This is the word *amemphomai*. It means "without blemish, without defect," and is therefore almost identical in meaning with the Hebrew *tamim*. This is especially clear in such a passage as 1 Peter 1:19, "but with the precious blood of Christ, a lamb *without blemish* or defect." Here Peter is using the word in precisely the same way *tamim* is used to describe the kind of animal that was acceptable for an offering in Leviticus. In Hebrews 9:14 a similar point is made when it is said, "How much more, then, will the blood of Christ, who through the eternal Spirit offered himself *unblemished* to God...." In other words, Christ made a "perfect" offering. There was no defect in what he offered to God.

The same thing can be said of human behavior. So, Paul calls upon the Thessalonians to bear witness that he conducted himself among them in a holy, just, and "blameless" manner (1 Thess. 2:10). There was no fault in his behavior toward them. The same thing is said of Zechariah and Elizabeth in Luke 1:6: they observed "all the Lord's commandments and regulations *blamelessly*." Paul can give the same testimony of himself as a Pharisee: he was "blameless" with respect to the Law (Philippians 3:6).[29]

When the word is applied to the kind of Christian character that the apostles expected in their converts, its import is very clear. It is especially interesting that a number of the references are associated with the idea of being made holy. So in Ephesians, both at the

---

[29]Three other Greek words are also used to describe human behavior which is above reproof. These are *anengkaleo, anepilambanomai* and *anaitios*. For some representative examples of the first two, see 1 Tim. 3:2, and 3:10. These and the several other occurrences in pastoral epistles are concerning the reputations of prospective Church leaders. They must be "without accusation." The third only appears in this sense in Matt. 12:6, 7.

beginning and at the end, Paul expresses his desire that his readers should be made holy and "blameless":

> For he chose us in him before the creation of the world to be holy and *blameless* in his sight [before him] (1:4).

> Husbands, love your wives, just as Christ loved the church and gave himself up for her to make her holy, cleansing her by the washing with water through the word, and to present her to himself as a radiant church, without stain or wrinkle or any other blemish, but holy and *blameless* (5:25-27).

Just as in the Old Testament, God's goal for us is that we should share his character without blemish or defect. Just as David could speak of walking before God in a way that was without defect, so every Christian believer, now that the Holy Spirit has come, can walk.

In Philippians 2:14-16a Paul makes it plain that he is not talking about a kind of holiness, or blamelessness, which is merely imputed to us as a kind of legal fiction. He says,

> Do everything without complaining or arguing, so that you may become *blameless* and pure, children of God *without fault* in a crooked and depraved generation, in which you shine like stars in the universe as you hold out the word of life. . . .

It is our reaction toward one another which Paul believes can be absolutely above reproach. We do not have to be motivated by selfish concerns as we deal with one another. We can manifest that "perfect love" which Jesus commanded and which John made one of the evidences of being a Christian.

The same thought appears again in Colossians 1:22. What was the purpose of Christ's death? Forgiveness and a place in heaven? No, God has reconciled us to himself for another purpose: "But now he has reconciled you by Christ's physical body through death to present you holy in his sight [before him], without blemish and free from accusation [*anengkleytos*]. . . ." As we have repeatedly said above, God's goal for us, and his purpose in revealing himself to us, is that we should be like him in a holy character which is as much like his as could possibly be expected given our human limitations. Here once again, Paul is confirming that this is the purpose of Christ's sacrifice.

It is especially in the book of 1 Thessalonians that we see Paul's concern for his converts, and we will look at that book in detail in the next chapter. But there are two occurrences of "blameless" here which should be noted in the present discussion. The first is found in 3:13 and the second in 5:23. In the first the apostle says

> May the Lord make your love increase and overflow for each other and for everyone else, just as ours does for you. May he strengthen [AV establish, cf. Psa. 51:10] your hearts so that you will be *blameless* and holy in the presence of our God and Father when our Lord Jesus comes with all his holy ones.

In the second reference we find:

> May God himself, the God of peace, sanctify you [make you holy] through and through [completely, *oloteleis*]. May your whole spirit, soul and body be kept *blameless* at the coming of our Lord Jesus Christ.

Again we find in both of these references the interconnection of holiness and a condition of being without fault or blemish. Nor is this a condition that is to apply only after Christ's coming. It is a condition that we are expected to have now and which will be in effect *until* Christ comes. In both cases we note that this effect is the result of the power of God, and is not in any way the result of our striving. But at the same time, this is a real condition that Paul wants to characterize us, his readers. Note also in the second of the two references, the reiterated concern for completeness. Paul does not envision a holiness that will be superficial or restricted to one area of our lives. Instead he is looking for a kind of transformation which will have its impact on everything we are and do. He asks that God will make us holy extensively, that is completely, and intensively, leaving no part of our being outside of his touch. The result of that touch, as Paul envisions it, is that we will be without defect, "blameless."

Nor is this concern that Christians will live out the holiness of God in a way that is fully complete restricted to Paul. Peter shows the same concern. Not only does he call his readers to be holy (1 Pet. 1:15-16) in a context which very clearly is calling for a certain kind of behavior and not merely speaking about a standing, he also calls them to "make every effort to be found spotless, blameless and at peace with him" (2 Pet. 3:14). Like Paul, Peter believes that it is possible for Christians to live a kind of life where no charge can be brought against them, either by humans or by God. Someone might say that the text only says "make every effort"; it does not say that this can actually be done. Again, as I said in the context of Romans, chapter 6, to give someone a command to do something you know is impossible for them is not only cynical it is cruel. Neither of those characteristics describes the New Testament writers. If they call upon us to do something, it must be because they believe that command is capable of fulfillment.

Jude shows the same confidence when in his closing he says, "To him who is able to keep you from falling and to present you before his glorious presence *without fault* and with great joy...." (24). Jude clearly believes that a Christian does not need to be constantly sinning. He believes that there is power in Christ which can keep us from that kind of behavior so that we can stand before God, all praise to him, in a condition of perfection, that is, with no defects.

The study undertaken in this chapter has shown how the New Testament has taken over the Old Testament concept to the extent that whereas a few persons in the Old Testament had that testimony that their lives before God were without defect—were perfect—now this is the expectation for all Christians. This kind of living is an expectation for all because the Holy Spirit, who was only available to a few in the Old Testament era, has now, through the sacrifice of Christ, become the possession of all. Thus, from the gospels throughout the epistles and into the Revelation, the words that were used to translate the Old Testament words for perfection are found being used regularly with regard to believers. They appear in commands, in exhortations and in prayers. Christ came in order that God might do what he intended from the beginning: share his character with us by taking up residence in us. He intends that no one would be able to lay any just charge against us: our sins of the past are under Christ's blood and by the power of the Holy Spirit we may grow up into the fullness of the measure of the stature of Christ, perfect and blameless. If this seems too breathtaking to be true, I can only ask that you review the texts again. Is this not the plain sense of what they are saying? If the reality they portray seems far from the day-to-day reality of the Christian Church, I can only ask which picture is the real one.

11

How to Experience
the Life of Holiness

If it is true that God's goal for our lives is that we shall share his character and live out his life, and if all Christians have received the Holy Spirit who makes such a life possible, why do so many Christians seem to fall so far short of the goal? This is a question that cannot be lightly set aside. As John Wesley was wont to say, if you find that experience does not accord with theology, it is probably the theology that is wrong! So, does the plain fact that many professing Christians (despite their good intentions otherwise) appear to be constantly defeated by sin mean that, whatever the Bible *seems* to be saying on the subject, it cannot mean what it seems? No it does not. What this inescapable fact means is that many, and perhaps most, Christians are living far below their privilege. A famous story tells of a poor man who dreamed of taking a journey on a great ocean liner. He saved his money carefully for many years and finally calculated that he had enough money to buy the ticket. But when everything had been added up he realized that he did not have enough money left over to pay for the kind of sumptuous meals he had heard they served on ocean liners. So he took what he had and bought a large box of soda crackers and some cheese and took it aboard with him. So when the rest of the passengers went to the dining room for their meals, this man stayed in his room and ate crackers and cheese, just counting himself fortunate to be having this experience at all. But on the last day afloat, he determined that he would have at least one of those wonderful meals, so he took all the money he had left, hoping it would be enough, and went to the dining room. Imagine his surprise and chagrin when he was told by the steward that they had been holding his place at the table all week because the price of the meals was included in the price of the ticket.

I am convinced that this old story accurately describes the state of far too many Christians. The life of the Spirit is theirs. That blessed condition where they can live lives of obedience, free from ravaging self-consciousness, joyously learning and doing the will of their heavenly Father is theirs. It was purchased for them on the Cross. The power of the Holy Spirit is in them ready to be unleashed to enable them to live lives which are blameless before God, lives which are without defect in God's sight. Yet they struggle on with their "crackers and cheese" when a sumptuous feast is spread and a place card with their name on it marks the place reserved for them.

Why is this the case? Because in God's economy you cannot possess what you do not have the faith to ask for. You cannot possess a love that is genuinely self-forgetful, that does not ask what it can get out of a relationship, unless you exercise faith to receive it. You cannot possess a heart that is wholly the possession of God unless you exercise faith for it. You cannot be absolutely faithful, even when it seems to be costing you too much, unless you exercise faith for it. Why this should be so is an important question which I want to leave to a later chapter. Here I want to show from the Bible that this is indeed the case, one that Paul in particular recognized very well. If his converts were to enjoy holy lives that were blameless, or perfect, before God, as he wanted them to do, then like the Israelites they needed to discover their need, discover the supply which was there to meet that need, and exercise the faith to bring the supply and the need together. This understanding can be seen in all Paul's letters to some extent, but it is especially clear in Ephesians and Colossians, and even more in 1 Thessalonians, to which I want to give major attention here.

1 Thessalonians

If Galatians is the earliest of Paul's letters that has been preserved for us, then 1 Thessalonians is the next-earliest. It was written back to the Thessalonian Christians from Corinth in the middle of the second missionary journey, at perhaps about 50 or 51 A.D., not many months after Paul's first visit to Thessalonica. As one of Paul's earliest preserved letters, it gives us excellent insight into Paul's most basic concerns for his converts in the early days of their Christian experience and in the early days of Paul's ministry.

The great apostle begins his letter in a way that would prove characteristic of him in later letters to other churches: with prayer and commendation. Here Paul commends the Thessalonians for the wonderful way they responded to his preaching (1:4-10). He knows that they are truly converted, both because of the tremendous conviction that the Holy Spirit laid upon them when he preached to them and because of the tremendous joy the Holy Spirit gave them when they believed. In fact, their remarkable faith in the good news Paul announced has become known everywhere. Paul does not need to tell people about it. They tell him! (1:8-9)

In chapter 2 Paul reminds them of his life-style among them. In particular, it was not motivated by any sort of selfishness. Paul's goal is not to gain the favor of men for himself; rather, his only goal is to please God (2:3-6). Paul and his companions went out of their way to make it clear that they were not using their ministry as a way of making money (2:7-9). In fact, the Thessalonians are witnesses that Paul's behavior was "holy, righteous, and blameless" among them "encouraging, comforting and urging" them "to live lives worthy of God who calls you into his kingdom and glory" (2:10-12). Unfortunately, this kind of unself-centered ministry has not characterized the Jews who have tried to prevent the mission to the Gentiles (2:15-16).

But Paul confesses, in spite of his confidence in the reality of what God had done among the Thessalonians, that he had desperately wanted to come back to visit them. He was afraid that the persecution they had suffered because of their Christian faith might have broken that faith (2:17-3:5). Finally, unable to come himself and unable to bear the suspense any longer, he had sent Timothy to visit and encourage them (3:2). Timothy has now returned with the welcome news that in spite of their trouble, their faith has remained strong and undaunted. Neither do they blame Paul for the things they have endured, but their love for him is as warm as ever (3:6). This is tremendously encouraging for Paul and he is thankful to God for the wonderful joy they have given him (3:7-9).

But now comes a word for which we are quite unprepared. We might expect Paul to say that he is relieved to learn that their faith is so strong because that means he need not undertake the arduous journey to come and see them. In fact, what he does say is that now he is praying night and day that he may come to them, and that God himself and the Lord Jesus will somehow make it possible (3:10-11). And why? To enjoy their wonderful faith, born in the fires of Spirit-given conviction and tempered in the white-hot fires of persecution? Not at all! Paul wants to come to them desperately, even more desperately than before, to "supply what is lacking in their faith" (3:10)! What is going on here? What is lacking in their faith? Everything in the book to this point has suggested that nothing is lacking in their faith.

But clearly Paul realizes that these people are now ready to take another step forward in faith. Now that it is clear they are not those plants Jesus spoke of that spring up quickly but are dried up by the sun or choked out by the thorns. It is time for them to take the next step. What is that step? We get a glimpse of it in 3:13-14. What does God have in store for these dear Thessalonian Christians if they will not try to manufacture it like the Galatian Christians thought they had to, but will believe Him for it? God can give them a whole new level of love; one which simply overflows the bounds of self, as they have seen it do in Paul (v. 12). God can so fix the control center of their lives on him that they will be holy and blameless before him when Jesus comes, whether that be tomorrow, or next year, or next century (v. 13). On this last point we get a glimpse of Paul's oblique approach to what was apparently an emerging problem in Thessalonica. The church there was getting absorbed in the fascinating questions surrounding Jesus' Second Coming (see 4:13-5:11; and 2 Thess. 2:1-16). They wished that Paul could come to them and settle some of their debates. But Paul says that what matters is not precisely when and how Jesus will come, important as those issues may be. Rather, what matters is what will be the condition of our lives when he does come. This is what exercises Paul so tremendously for them, and this is why he would like so much to come and see them. That not being possible (apparently), he settles for this letter, telling them there is more to believe for, and telling them what that is. This subject takes up the remainder of the book.

What are the things that are lacking in the faith of the Thessalonians? What is it for which they have not yet believed? In a word, and a big one, it is "sanctification" or being made holy (4:3). Paul says that he has told them before of the necessity for holy living, and that indeed, they are doing so. But Paul now "asks and urges" them "in the Lord Jesus" that these characteristics should abound in their lives 4:1-2.[30] The fact that this has been put into the context of lack of faith shows that Paul is not merely giving them a "pep talk" and encouraging them to try a little harder. If God's will that his people be holy in their behavior is to be realized, it is not, above all, a matter of trying harder. That is "the flesh" about which Paul had just warned the Galatians, and about which he was shortly to warn the Romans. No, if we are to be the holy people that God has longed for from the beginning, it must be a matter of his Spirit's doing that work in us, and that is a matter for faith. This is precisely the point Paul was making in Galatians when he said that if we live by the Spirit we will not gratify "the flesh" (5:16). In our own strength and selfish desires we can never live God's holy life. But if we live in the Spirit, we will produce that fruit which the Old Covenant required, but could not produce because of that twisted, self-centered spirit within us which Paul calls "the flesh" (5:17-6:10).

---

[30] The NIV, by reversing the order of the clauses, has lessened the sense of urgency that was communicated when the exhortation came first in the sentence, as it does in the Greek. See NRSV and NKJV.

This is what Paul longs to tell the Thessalonians now that they are ready to hear it. Before they had undergone persecution and had to pay a high price for their faith, they may have thought, like the Israelites did, that living a holy life, the life of God, was no big problem. Now they know it is not quite so simple. Now they have come up against "the flesh" in all its stubborn resilience. Now they are ready to hear that the holy life is entered into on precisely the same basis as the Christian experience is entered into—"nothing in my hands I bring, simply to thy Cross I cling." Why do so many Christians live beneath their means? Because they have never believed God to "crucify their sinful flesh" (Gal. 5:25) and make them like him. That's what Paul was afraid the Thessalonians might fail to do, and that's why he was so desperate to visit them.

What were the areas which would be dealt with if the Thessalonians would exercise faith? The first is sexuality (4:3-8). Over and over again, our Enemy uses our sexuality to defeat us. Although this desire is not as elemental as the others (a starving man has little sexual desire), it is infinitely more complex. All our needs for belonging, for being wanted, for surrender, for mastery are tangled up with this physical desire. And unless God does something for us we cannot do for ourselves, we will be mastered and destroyed by our sexuality. Paul longs to tell his Thessalonian brothers and sisters that the same sort of faith which they once exercised to receive the grace of forgiveness, they can now exercise to make them masters over their sexual desires.

A second area of the Thessalonians' lives that Paul recognized needed the sanctifying grace of God was "brotherly love" (4:9-10). Like them, we do not need much exhortation in this area. We know we should do this. If we have been Christians very long we have heard more than enough about it. But the question is, how? Simply knowing we should love others is not enough. Somehow we need to discover a dynamic which will enable us to overcome the "flesh" which turns everything back upon itself and prevents us from freely giving ourselves away without always questioning whether we will get our love back with interest or not. This was what Paul was talking about in 3:12 when he prayed that *the Lord* would make their love increase and abound. It is as we allow the Holy Spirit to fill us first with his unconditional love for us and then with his power to love the unlovely that we will find ourselves able to love "perfectly" as Jesus commanded (Matt. 5:48) and as John explained (1 John 4:7-21).

Closely related to this is the issue of the appropriate attitude towards others, whether they be nominally over us as leaders or whether they "under" us as those who are weaker than we (5:12-15). With regard to leaders, the "flesh" hates to be in submission to anyone, and it makes little difference whether the leadership is enlightened or oppressive. But the self-centered and self-serving attitude which "flesh" expresses also understands that open rebellion is not always well received, even by one's peers. So the typical response is a flurry of compliments to the leader's face coupled with a cynical sniping behind the leader's back. This is if the leader is strong. If the leader is weak, the "flesh" can express itself in public sulkiness and private undercutting of whatever the leader is attempting. None of us who have been in Christian circles long can deny that this sort of behavior is present among Christians. What is to be done? God's will is that we should be holy, and this kind of behavior is anything but holy. Paul wants to tell his Thessalonian friends that they can exercise faith to be relieved of the need to exalt themselves at the expense of others. We can reach a state of grace where we do not need to bring people down so that we can feel better about ourselves.

That same state of grace can bring us to the place where we do not grade the significance of persons on the basis of what they can do for us. The "flesh" dismisses as unimportant those who cannot advance its own cause. But Paul envisions for the Thessalonians a condition of heart where they will be able to forget the question "What can these people do for me?" and instead ask, "What has God given me for these, the idle, the timid, the weak?" (5:14).

Yet another area which concerns Paul for his friends is the area of self-discipline (4:11-12). Like our sexuality, our desire for pleasure and diversion can very easily undercut all our strong intentions to live lives wholly given over to our Savior. It is not enough to make new vows, or to "turn over a new leaf." We must exercise faith in the Holy Spirit's power to deal with that self-serving spirit radically, to "crucify" it, as Paul put it in Galatians 5:24. The indiscipline is not the problem. It is only a symptom, a symptom of that twisted spirit, that corrupted imagination, which Old Testament believers had discovered in themselves. This was why Paul was so passionately concerned to get the message to the Thessalonians. As Christians, they needed to know, just as the Galatians did, that within themselves was already the power of the Spirit, waiting to be unleashed through a new act of faith. The Holy Spirit would enable them to fulfill the perfect will of God (as Paul spoke of it in Romans 12:2) making them a holy people. None of this is to suggest that diversion is wrong. God made us so that we cannot be at our best without some diversion and change of pace. But so long as we are in the grip of the self-serving and self-pleasing power of the "flesh," that need for diversion is corrupted, becoming an end in itself. When we have been set free under the lordship of Christ, we find this need no longer ruling us, but we rule it. It has now become clean and we can use it cleanly and with joy. Here is another paradox of the gospel. So long as we refuse to surrender to the Spirit absolutely, thinking that we will rule ourselves, then our desires rule us with an addictive, unclean force. But when we make that further surrender of faith, giving absolute control to the Spirit who is in us, we discover that our desires are now subservient to us, and we have a power over them which we never had when we tried to arrogate power to ourselves.

Interestingly, Paul does not tell his converts just to forget the issues surrounding the Second Coming and concentrate on allowing the Spirit to make them a holy people. Too often we swing to extremes like this. We think everything has to do with getting the right understanding of the facts of our faith, and that how we live is quite secondary. Or, seeing the fallacy of that point of view, we fall into the opposite ditch, thinking that if we will learn how to live loving, self-surrendered, self-disciplined, pure lives, it doesn't really matter what we believe. The truth is that neither of these poles can be ignored. If Paul does not want his people to be so fascinated by the Second Coming that they fail to realize the holiness which was God's goal in saving them, neither does he want them to fall into the trap of thinking that "it really doesn't matter much what you believe if your heart's right." So in 4:13-5:11 he carefully instructs them about the facts of the Second Coming. Right living rests upon right doctrine, and right doctrine is not right unless it results in right living. Paul shows the truth of this aphorism already in 5:1-11, where he begins to take the thread of his thought back to the present. He says that the issue is not when Christ will return, but whether we will be ready to meet him when he comes. We will show our readiness by being "alert and self-controlled" (v. 6) manifesting faith, love, and hope (v. 8).

It is this overall manner of life that Paul sees as the final area where the faith which Paul wants to convey to his readers will have its effect. When we have believed God to set us free from the "flesh," enabling us to be the holy people he desires, our whole approach to life will be different (5:16-22). Underneath everything there will be a joy which circumstances may disturb, but cannot destroy (v. 16). This is so because it is the joy of having found one's true rest and of being in the way for which one was designed. Likewise, because the Holy Spirit has complete control, prayer becomes simply a way of life; our talking things over with the manager, as it were (v. 17). Thankfulness will be our normal attitude (v. 18) because, unlike the days when we were dominated by the "flesh," we will no longer be thinking of all that we deserve that we never get. Rather, we will be astonished that we, who deserve nothing but eternal damnation, have been made the very heirs of heaven. When the "flesh" rules, it is constantly chafing at the "unreasonable" demands of God; not that his demands are unreasonable, but that the unsurrendered self finds all commands unreasonable. Now having exercised faith to allow the Spirit of Christ to fill us, we are amazed that God gives so much and asks so little. Has God changed? No, we have changed, with the result that we now see things as they are, and are filled with gratitude.

Verses 19-22 describe the kind of spiritual balance that is possible for persons who are wholly given over to God through the Spirit. On the one hand, they are very sensitive to his leading and inspiration. They are eager and willing to hear what he has to say from any source.

But at the same time they are not naive and gullible. Everything claiming to have originated with the Spirit does not necessarily originate there. Through responsiveness to him, they learn to distinguish good from evil and to develop their powers of discernment.

But isn't it possible I am reading too much into chapters 4 and 5? After all, the admonitions about sexuality, love, self-discipline, etc. that we have just been considering are not all that different from what is found in most of Paul's other letters. But perhaps we ought to think of what he says in his other letters in the light of this one and not vice versa. For verses 23-24, by their very explicit reversion to what was said in 3:11-13 seem to give a clear context for how Paul wants us to understand what lies between 3:13 and 5:23. That is, 4:1-5:22 is the detail Paul has in mind when he speaks of his longing for God to make the Thessalonians a holy people without any defects. Paul's expression here is, if anything, even more pointed than it was at the beginning of the passage.

> May God himself, the God of peace, sanctify you through and through [*oloteleis*, "completely," "entirely"]. May your whole spirit, soul and body be kept blameless [*amemptos*] at the coming of our Lord Jesus Christ. The one who calls you is faithful and he will do it.

Again Paul emphasizes that this is God's work, not theirs. To be sure, they must exercise faith, they must believe God to do it, but it is God's work. So the exhortations in 4:1-5:22 are not merely exhortations. They are calls for the Thessalonians to believe God to do these things in them. Then he expresses his desire that God may make them completely holy. That is, he is not asking for something superficial or partial. He believes that God can do something in these people which will make them Christlike (for this is what it means to be holy) in every aspect of their lives. If there were any question about what he means by such a statement, he explains it by saying that he wants them to be without defect in spirit, soul, and body from now until Christ comes! What a wonderful hope! But it is more than a hope; it is Paul's settled confidence. "The one who calls you is faithful and he will do it" (5:24). So there is no excuse for anyone to say, "Oh well, I just don't think I can live up to a standard like that." Of course we can't; the whole Old Testament teaches us that. But that is not the point. The point is: does God want to do this in us? Surely the answer is yes. And is he able to do it? Again the answer is yes. But now comes the frightening caveat. Yes, he is able to do what he wants if we will believe him to do it. Tragically, there are many people today who simply will not believe God to make them holy. That is what Paul was afraid might happen to the Thessalonians, and that is why his longing was so intense to tell them about the wonderful possibilities that are already theirs in Christ.[31]

Colossians

Paul does the same sort of thing in the book of Colossians as he does in 1 Thessalonians. I will not go into as much detail with this material because I simply want to use it to show that what Paul is doing in 1 Thessalonians is not unique to that book. In Colossians Paul is apparently trying to resolve a dispute between those who say that it is what you know that makes you a Christian and those who say it is what you do (2:6-23). For convenience's sake these two groups have been labeled "Gnostics" (from the Greek word for knowledge, *gnosis*) and "the Judaizers" (those who believed that salvation required both faith and keeping the Old Testament ceremonial law). In fact, Paul says, neither of those approaches is any good because they cannot control "the flesh." The New International Version translates "flesh" here with "sensual indulgence." Unfortunately, this is no better than "sinful nature" which is used in Romans and elsewhere. If that phrase obscured some of the connotations of the word, this one limits it too far. It is not merely sensual indulgence that spiritual knowledge and

---

[31]While almost all commentators on 1 Thessalonians recognize that chapters 4 and 5 are dealing with ethical matters, few recognize the significance of this material's being bracketed by the prayers for sanctification in 3:11-13 and 5:23-24. Two which make some motions in that direction are: *E. Best, A Commentary on the First and Second Epistles to the Thessalonians*, Black's New Testament Commentaries, London: Adams and Black, 1972, and J. Elias, *1&2 Thessalonians*, Believers Church Bible Commentary, eds. E. Martens and W. Swartley, Scottdale, Pa.: Herald Press, 1995.

rigorous piety cannot control. What they cannot control is that self-will within us which is determined to have its own way and please itself at all costs. Sensual indulgence is a manifestation of that attitude, but it is the attitude itself that prevents many Christians from experiencing the holiness which is theirs by birthright through Christ.

So we ask Paul, if neither of those approaches is the answer to our most fundamental problem, what is? His answer is remarkably similar to that which we found in Romans 6. It is our identification with Christ (3:1-4). This is what makes us truly Christian: our experience of the Christ-life within us. In Him our "flesh" died and we have been resurrected to a whole new "heavenly" attitude. We have died to pride in our intellectual attainment or to the ritualistic evidences of our piety. Those things have no power to control our lusts for pleasure and possessions and power (3:5); nor do they have any power over the fury (all too often an impotent one) which wracks us when our will is crossed (3:8); nor can they make us true in the face of the temptation to present ourselves as what we are not (3:9). All of those are "the flesh." And the only thing that can control that is the Spirit of Christ living in us.

What is the evidence of that Spirit? We see it in verses 12-17. Interestingly, everything here is described in relational terms. Holiness that can only be lived out in isolation, in what used to be called "the prayer closet," or in the monastic cell, is of no interest to Paul at all. When Christ rules our lives, when his Spirit fills us, when our "flesh" has been crucified, the evidence is seen in how we treat one another. And that is how it should be, for it is in God's treatment of persons that the unique qualities of his holy character are seen. So among God's people there is "compassion, kindness, humility, gentleness and patience" (v. 12). There is forgiveness (v. 13), love (v. 14), peace and gratitude (v. 15), and harmonious worship in which all participate in the teaching of the word and in the raising of grateful hymns (v. 16). And all of this is done through the authority (the name) of Christ with gratitude (v. 17), because none of it would be possible without his indwelling presence (John 15).

But when we look closely at this discussion, we see Paul expressing himself in what appear to be contradictory terms. On the one hand, he says that his hearers have died to a form of life where they try to project themselves forward, and where they try to outdo others; one in which desire and anger and lying rule the life (2:20; 3:3). Instead, they have been raised to a new life with Christ (3:1). Similarly, he says, "you have taken off your old self [32] with its practices and put on a new self, which is being renewed in knowledge in the image of its Creator" (3:9b-10). In other words Paul speaks of these changes as already having happened. The Colossian Christians are *now* dead to the old self life, and they have *already* put off the old clothing and have put on the new. But then, very strangely, the apostle commands his readers to die (v. 5) and to put on new clothing (v. 12). What is going on? Would we ever command a corpse to die, or a person dressed in new clothes to put on new clothes? Surely not. Yet that seems to be what Paul is doing here.

Is it not that Paul is speaking of potential and the realization of that potential? He is saying that when a person accepts Christ by faith then all of the power of the Holy Spirit to make that person holy becomes theirs. In potential they are dead to the "flesh" and all its works, its pride, its touchiness, its self-absorption. In that same potential they are alive to a self-forgetful compassion, humility, etc. But what does Paul mean when he now commands us to die, to put on our new clothes? Is it not precisely the same as in 1 Thessalonians? The potential for the holy life must be released by faith. It is not something that is entered into automatically by becoming a Christian. So Paul entreats his Colossian converts, "Let loose all the wonderful potential that was given you when you accepted Christ. Do so in an act of self-renunciation (death) and in an act of acceptance and faith (put on), so that the holiness which Christ came to give you may be yours. Claim by faith what is already yours." There is nothing here of striving and struggling and constantly falling short of something which is outside of ourselves. Rather, we are invited to unlock a door in the new

---

[32]This concept of the old self (AV old man) is synonymous with "the flesh" as is seen in its uses in Rom. 6:6 (compare with Gal. 5:24) and Eph. 4:22.

house that has been given us and to find there all the furnishings already in place.

Ephesians

The same ideas are found in Ephesians. In 1:4 Paul declares that God's purpose in choosing us was that we might be "holy and blameless" before Him. We are to be for "the praise of his glory" (1:12), "created in Christ Jesus to do good works" (2:10), "created to be like God in true righteousness and holiness" (4:24). Now we who were once "dead in transgressions" are "alive with Christ" (2:5). We were

> taught, with regard to your former way of life, to put off your old self, which is being corrupted by its deceitful desires; to be made new in the attitude of your minds; and to put on the new self, created to be like God in true righteousness and holiness (4:22-24).

Yet, in his unusual prayer in chapter 3 (normally his prayers are at the beginning of his letters) Paul prays that the Ephesians might so experience the Spirit within them that Christ may dwell in their hearts by faith, with the result that they might know by experience how boundless the love of Christ is and that they might be filled with the fullness of God (3:16-19). And Paul is confident that God can do all this through "*his power that is at work within us*" (3:20).

Once again we ask what is going on. Is Christ in their hearts or not? Have they put off the "old self" or not? And once again I suggest that Paul is speaking about potential and the realization of that potential. Christ *does* dwell in them, but not in the sense that he can if they will allow the power of the Spirit that *is* in them to have full sway. They have been taught of the necessity to put off the "old man." Now by faith they must do it. They were created in Christ for good works. Now they must allow Christ to crucify that old self in order that the love of Christ may flow through them without any boundaries. You're dead, now die! You are alive, now live! We may think of Ezekiel's Valley of Dry Bones. The bones have been rejoined, the skeletons have been covered with living flesh, and yet the bodies are inert. What must happen? The breath of the Spirit must blow into their nostrils. Then that which is alive will live!

So we return to the question with which we opened this chapter. If it is true that God intends for us to live lives of blameless holiness; if he expects our sacrifice to be perfect before him, why are so few Christians living on that plane? I have tried to show that it is because that plane of Christian living is not automatic. It is entered into by a further act of self-renunciation and of faith. This is what Paul's epistles from Galatians onward show.

But why should this be the case? If Christ died and rose again in order to make it possible for the Holy Spirit to live in us, and if all who truly believe do have the Spirit living in them, why aren't Christians fully holy from the moment of their conversion? The answer lies in the nature of faith. You cannot believe for something you do not know you need. And the fact is that before accepting Christ we are as ignorant of our true natures as the Hebrews were at the foot of Mount Sinai. How can we ask God to crucify that self-will that is so adamantly opposed to his when we do not know we have it? How can we ask the Holy Spirit to cleanse us of that "fleshly" attitude that is determined to do everything for itself and by itself and to trample any who get in its way if we have never come face to face with it before? So when we are asked as baby Christians whether we are going to make Jesus the Lord of our lives and live wholly for him, we answer just as blithely, and just as sincerely, as the Hebrews did at Sinai, "Of course!"

Little do we know! And why should we? Never before have we ourselves tried to cross that stubborn will. Others could perhaps tell us about what they saw in us, but it made no impression. So it is on a sailboat traveling with the wind: the passengers would say, "Ah, there is no wind blowing" even though that is the fastest point of the boat's travel. They feel no wind because they are moving at the same speed as the wind. Oh, but let them try to sail across that wind. The boat is actually traveling slower than it was before, but now it feels like a veritable windstorm is hurling them about. So it is with us. When we are living for our "flesh," our "old self," we are not aware of it at all, because we are traveling with it. It is only when we begin to try to go against it in response to the Spirit of Christ within us that we begin to discover, like the Hebrews did, that there is something within us which is opposed to Christ. Paul says much the same thing in Romans 7 when he says that he did not know he was a sinner until he began to try to obey the law and found that while he could obey it outwardly, he could not do so from the heart (vss. 7-9).

This is the critical moment in the Christian experience. It will come sooner in some cases, later in others. One kind of experience may trigger the crisis in some kinds of people, another kind may trigger it in others. Happy the person who does come to it. Sad the person whose spiritual senses are so dull or who has never had a thoroughly biblical grounding and cannot recognize the symptoms when they present themselves. It often involves a career decision where God's will is revealed and the self demands another way. It may involve a love affair, or a habit, or a diversion. It may be the call to take a stand for righteousness that we know (or fear) will result in persecution. It may be the ugly realization that we are determined to have our way in a conflict even though someone else's way is better. But there we are. God's will is clear, and self-will says, "Never!" Now what? Paul's answer comes ringing across the centuries, "I pray night and day that I might come to you and supply what is lacking in your faith." "You're dead, now die!" "By the Spirit put to death the deeds of the flesh." "May God himself, the God who puts things together, make you completely holy. May every part of you, inside and out, be put beyond reproach until Jesus comes."

The sad picture of so many Christians struggling to be like Christ in their own strength, and always falling short of the standard, or of others who have given up and are living lives of pride, greed, and self-indulgence, claiming Christ's forgiveness, is not only sad; it is tragic. It is tragic because it does not need to be the case. If the full gospel were understood and preached with clarity there could be a new day of righteousness dawning about us instead of a deepening twilight of unbelief and cynicism.

12
Holiness and Sin

But if we are to understand and appropriate what the Bible offers to us in the realm of holy living, it is imperative that we understand sin as the Bible does. A century ago the idea of holy living was an essential part of experiential Christianity in Great Britain and the United States. But that idea has fallen into its present low repute because of the failure at various levels to communicate accurately. As a result, many who sincerely sought the power of the Holy Spirit to make them holy people felt that the promises did not match the reality either in themselves or in those around them. They saw people who claimed to be sinless who seemed to be harsh, censorious, and self-righteous. They found in themselves feelings and reactions that they thought holy people would not have. As a result of these kinds of experiences many despaired of ever being the holy people they wanted to be. Some became cynical and hard, but the majority simply settled for the comfortable idea that God does not expect us to actually be holy, only to be accounted so through the blood of Christ.

A clearer understanding of the biblical view of sin would have gone far to prevent this tragic state of affairs. With such an understanding we will recognize that the biblical call to holiness is not something which is contrary to human nature, even redeemed human nature, but is entirely in keeping with who we are and what we may realistically become.

Without Sin?

At the outset we must ask whether the claim to be able to live lives which are blameless in holiness, ones which are above sin, is even in keeping with Scripture. Is this not a claim to sinlessness, something that 1 John 1:8-10 seems to speak strongly against? The brief answer to the question is "no," but before we can answer the question more fully, we need to look at that passage in 1 John, coupling with it 1:6-7 and 2:1-2:

> If we claim to have fellowship with him yet walk in the darkness, we lie and do not live by the truth. But if we walk in the light, as he is in the light, we have fellowship with one another, and the blood of Jesus, his Son, purifies us from all sin. If we claim to be without sin, we deceive ourselves and the truth is not in us. If we confess our sins, he is faithful and just and will forgive us our sins and purify us from all unrighteousness. If we claim we have not sinned, we make him out to be a liar and his word has no place in our lives. My dear children, I write this to you so that you will not sin. But if anybody does sin, we have one who speaks to the Father in our defense—Jesus Christ, the Righteous One. He is the atoning sacrifice for our sins, and not for ours but for the sins of the whole world.

We need to add to this 3:4-9:

> Everyone who commits sin is guilty of lawlessness; sin is lawlessness. You know that he was revealed to take away sins, and in him there is no sin. No one who abides in him sins; no one who sins has either seen him or known him. Little children, let no one deceive you. Everyone who does what is right is righteous, just as he is righteous. Everyone who commits sin is a child of the devil; for the devil has been sinning from the beginning. The Son of God was revealed for this purpose, to destroy the works of the devil. Those who have been born of God do not sin, because God's seed abides in them; they cannot sin, because they have been born of God. (NRSV)

Whatever these two passages mean, they mean it in the light of the other. Neither one can be legitimately interpreted in such a way as to negate what the other is saying. Clearly the second of these is entirely in keeping with Romans 6. The thought of Christians continuing to live in known sin while claiming the redemptive blood of Christ is simply horrifying to John. Furthermore, he makes it crystal clear that it will not do to separate *being* righteous from *doing* righteousness. He says flatly that those who *do* righteousness *are* righteous, and that is that. He will not allow us to say that Christ has made us righteous even though we continue to do what is wrong. These words have terrified many young (and some not-so-young) Christians with their absolutistic flavor, so we can understand why the New International Version has tried to soften them with such translations as "No one who lives in him keeps on sinning" in place of "No one who abides in him sins" (v. 6), or "he cannot go on sinning," for "they cannot sin" (v. 10). But these kinds of changes are only cosmetic. A thoughtful reading of any faithful translation must yield the same truth. A Christian cannot live in known sin and remain in a saving relationship with Christ. The two are simply incompatible. Sin is of the Devil; righteousness is of Christ. The person who sins belongs to the Devil. If a person is born of God they cannot live in sin.

This must form the backdrop of any responsible interpretation of 1:8-10. These verses cannot be so interpreted as to cancel out 3:4-10 (or, for that matter, 1:5-7 and 2:1-6). We do not interpret the book by three verses. Rather, we interpret the verses by the plain sense of the book. 1 John 1:6–2:5 forms a single thought unit in which the apostle offers the first installment of the first of his three tests of the Christian faith: obedience, love, and belief. Here he says, as he does again in 3:4-10 and in 5:2-3, that the first mark of a Christian is a life of complete obedience to God and thus one of complete righteousness. He says that the person who says that they can live with God and in sin at the same time is a liar (1:5-6; 2:4). He says that his purpose in writing is that Christians not sin (2:1), and that in those who do obey God's word "the love of God has reached perfection (*teteleiotai*)" (NRSV), ("God's love is truly made complete" NIV[33]). What is it to love God

---

[33]It is unfortunate that the NIV translators in this example of their attempt to minimize perfection language wherever possible have obscured the direct connection of this passage with 4:17-18. The text says that it is possible for our love for God to be perfected in obedience, and this helps us to understand what 4:17-18 are talking about.

perfectly, completely, without a defect? It is to obey him! But we must not overlook the fact that John allows that a Christian, living and walking in God's light, might yet commit a sin. In such a case, the blood of Christ will avail for such a person, and fellowship will be restored.

It is in the light of all of this , then, that we must ask ourselves what John means to convey in verses 8-10 of chapter 1. Is he saying that Christians sin all the time and that if they say anything else they are liars? How could he be saying that, when he has so clearly said that Christians do not sin? How could he be saying that when he has just said we must either walk in the darkness or in the light and that we cannot be in both at the same time? How could he be saying that when he says that a person who says he knows God while disobeying him is a liar ? To do this would be to involve the writer in an impossible contradiction, not merely within his letter, but even within the same paragraph. So how can we reconcile these statements? I believe two things must be said. The first is relatively brief, but the second will return us to the question that opened this chapter and will occupy our attention for the rest of the chapter.

First, I believe that John is speaking somewhat parenthetically in verses 8-10. This is supported by the similarity between 1:6-7 and 2:1. In both of those places he says that we cannot live in sin, but he also says that if we are seeking to obey God and live for him and we do commit a sin, the blood of Christ is sufficient to cleanse us and restore us to fellowship. Between these reiterations John deals with a side issue, which was probably prevalent among some then, and continues to be heard even today. This is the protest of the person, too often an unbelieving churchgoer, who says that he or she is not a sinner and has never done anything which might require any "bucket of blood" to be poured out for them. That's right, they agree, a "Christian" shouldn't sin, and they personally do not and never have. John responds strongly to such an idea. Anyone who says they do not need the forgiveness of God is living in self-deception (v. 8). Furthermore, to say that we have never sinned is to make God a liar, for his word tells us un- mistakably that all of us have sinned and are in need of a savior (v. 10).

No indeed, the way to a life of victory over sin is not to begin by denying that we are sinners! Rather, we must begin by confessing our sins and our sinfulness. Then we will find the forgiveness of our sins and the cleansing that will together make possible the life of righteousness to which John (and all the other apostles) are calling us (v. 9). This, it seems to me, is the most natural way to understand the passage, one that does not involve John in an irreconcilable self-contradiction.[34]

Sin—A Matter of Will and Intent

We turn now to a second and more complicated issue which is raised by this passage. This discussion is necessitated not so much by 1:8-10 as it is by the verses on either side of them. John has bluntly said that it is impossible for a Christian to be "in the light" and "in the darkness" at the same time. Later, he even more bluntly says that Christians "do not sin," indeed, that they "cannot." But in 1:7 he clearly envisions the necessity of a person who is "walking in the light," that is, obeying God completely and loving him perfectly (2:5), being continuously cleansed from sin, and in 2:1 he speaks even more explicitly about the possibility of a Christian committing sin and so needing Christ's advocacy as the atoning sacrifice for sin.

How are we to understand statements like these? The first thing which they clearly underline is this: If John says that one who has been born of God "cannot sin," he does not mean that it becomes impossible for one born of God to sin. Clearly, he believes that the possibility of sin remains so long as we are alive. If it was possible for Adam and Eve to sin, it is possible for the Christian on earth to sin, in whatever state of grace they may find themselves. So what *does* he mean? Surely he means that it is impossible for a person born of

---

[34]It must be observed that almost all modern commentators chose to resolve the apparent contradiction in the opposite way, asserting that since 1:8-10 says that Christians sin, therefore 3:4-10 cannot mean what they seem to. See for instance, Stephen S. Smalley, *1,2,3 John*, Word Biblical Commentary 51, eds. D. Hubbard, G. Barker, Waco, Tex.: Word Books, 1984, pp. 159-176. A more satisfactory treatment is found in I. H. Marshall, *The Epistles of John*, New International Commentary on the New Testament, ed. F. F. Bruce, Grand Rapids: Eerdmans, 1978, pp. 175-188.

God to live in continuing intentional sin.[35] Whenever sin is revealed, we need to confess it and repent of it *then* and our fellowship can be continuous.

But there is something more going on here, and it has its roots in the Old Testament. In the Old Testament we see that there are two kinds of sin. The first is defined for us in Genesis 3. Sin is a willful transgression of the known command of God. Adam and Eve did not sever their relationship with God by accidentally cutting down the wrong tree. Nor did they do so by eating the fruit in ignorance. They brought tragedy upon the whole race by doing something that God had explicitly commanded them not to do. Moreover, they knew what God had said; they could not plead forgetfulness. This is an extremely important point. In pagan religions sin against the gods is almost never a sin against the gods' revealed will, for the simple reason that the will of the gods is hardly ever revealed in terms which are clear and understandable. But in the Bible, this is what sin at its root is all about: God's will for the way we live our lives with Him and with one another has been clearly revealed. Again and again, when the prophets convict their people of sin, it is in terms of what God had revealed in his Word.

This is the kind of sin which the Old Testament calls "sin with a high hand." The image is of a person who had been told not to do something shaking his or her fist over their head and saying, "I don't care what you want, I'm going to do it anyway." We find a good example of this in Numbers 15:30-36. The principle is stated in verses 30-31, and this is followed by an example in verses 32-36. The principle is this:

> 'But anyone who sins defiantly [*with a high hand*], whether native-born or alien, blasphemes the LORD, and that person must be cut off from his people. Because he has despised the LORD's word and broken his commands, that person must surely be cut off; his guilt remains on him.'

---

[35]So although the NIV is being interpretive when it translates 3:6 as "No one who lives in him *keeps on sinning*," it does capture the correct sense.

The example that follows has to do with a man found gathering wood on the Sabbath day. There was no atonement for what he had done. He was stoned to death outside the camp on the command of God to Moses. There is a chilling similarity here to the deaths of Nadab and Abihu. Like them, this man knew perfectly clearly what God's command was, but he decided that his way was better. On a larger scale, the entire preceding chapter in Numbers, the 14th, is an example of "sin with a high hand." God told his people to enter the promised land, but they refused to obey him. They thought they knew better than he, and that such an entry was impossible. Then, incredibly, when they learned that they would die in the wilderness of this offense, they decided they *would* enter the land even after Moses told them God was not with them and that they would fail! This is the sin or lawlessness; that which, according to John, the Devil seeks to foment, and that which his children practice. It is also, he says, that which Jesus came to do away with and that which those born of God do not practice.

We may give thanks that although the fates of Nadab and Abihu and this man (along with Achan [Josh. 7] and Uzzah [2 Sam. 6:1-7] and Ananias and Sapphira [Acts 5:1-11]) were perfectly just, they do not describe God's normal way of acting. In the timeless words of Archbishop Cranmer, "His property is always to have mercy." According to John (and Paul), Christians simply do not commit this sort of sin, but if, once in a great while, they should, God does not normally bring just sentence upon them instantly. He gives them the opportunity to repent and be restored, as he did to many in Israel. But the point here is that John and all the other apostles tell us that Christians don't need to do that any more. If it is possible for a Christian *to* sin, that is, to transgress the known law of God, the good news is that it is possible for a Christian *not to* sin. We do not need to live in rebellion against the One who loved us to the Cross, we do not need to break the heart of the Father who longs to give us the best. We do not need to sin in this sense of the word. If only Christians could get hold of this truth; if only they would believe God to do in them what they cannot do in themselves.

But this is clearly not all that is in John's mind. What is he thinking of when he says that when we walk in the light, the blood of Jesus "cleanses us from all sin" (1:7, NRSV)? This does not sound like what he is talking about in 2:1, where the implication is that an isolated act has broken fellowship and needs Christ's advocacy for restoration. Here what seems to be implied is a continuous cleansing for one who is not stepping out of the light of God's presence and fellowship. What is this? What cleansing is needed if we are not consciously disobeying God's commands?

Again it is the Old Testament which helps us to understand what is in the apostle's thinking.[36] While it is true that "sin rightly so-called"[37] is a willful transgression of the known law of God, that does not exhaust the Old Testament understanding. Again we may turn to Numbers 15 for an explanation of this point. Although that sinful generation would not be allowed to enter the promised land, that would not nullify God's promises. An evidence of this is the way chapter 15 begins, "The LORD spoke to Moses, saying: Speak to the Israelites and say to them: When you come into the promised land which you are to inhabit...." (vv. 1-2). Isn't that interesting? That generation would not come into that land. Yet the Israel of which they were a part would do so. God had promised. In that context God gives some additional instructions about the ways they should worship him in the land (vv. 3-21). Then comes the particular material we are interested in. God says that if anyone should "unintentionally fail to observe all these commandments" (v. 22) there are particular offerings which must be given either for the congregation as a whole (vv. 23-26) or for an individual (vv. 27-29). Even though the sin was un-intentional, atonement still had to be offered for it. I believe this is the sense of what John is saying in 1 John 1:7. Even though we are walking

---

[36]This should hardly surprise us. The Old Testament was the thought world of all the writers of the New Testament. Though they wrote in Greek and were undoubtedly influenced by that thought world, their native air was the Old Testament and the Hebraic way of thinking.

[37]This is a quote from John Wesley.

in the light and are not guilty of willful transgression of the known law of God, we will of necessity be falling short of the perfect righteousness of God and are thus in need of atonement. Why do I say "of necessity"? Because of our imperfect knowledge and our inherited fallibility. A good example of this latter feature is to be found of the story of Joseph's sale to the Midianites in Genesis 37. Reuben had planned to thwart his brothers' murderous jealousy. He succeeded in getting them not to kill Joseph outright, but to put him down into a dry cistern. Later he intended to come back and set him free. But in the meantime the Midianite traders had come by and the other brothers had seen a good opportunity not only to get rid of Joseph, but to make some money in the bargain. So when Reuben came back, Joseph was gone. His cry gives us some sense of his desolation, "And I, where shall I go?" (37:30, author's translation). He had failed his brother. He had not intended to, but he had. He did not want to sell his brother, but now by his failure, he had unwittingly participated in that very thing.

We may choose a more contemporary example for sin through lack of knowledge. Suppose something has happened in your past that has left you especially sensitive in some area of your life. I know nothing of this and make some remark that touches that area and hurts you deeply. I did not intend to hurt you, but I did. I have not willfully transgressed God's known law. But I have sinned unintentionally. My insensitive actions have hurt you, and if you tell me so, I need to ask your forgiveness and God's. If I do so, then there is never a break in my fellowship with God. And if you do not tell me what has happened, the blood of Christ cleanses me in my ignorance and permits me to continue walking in his light. If this is what those who stand in the Reformed tradition are talking about when they speak of sinning "daily in thought, deed and word" and thereby needing the atoning blood of Christ to be applied constantly, I agree with them most heartily. It is on this basis that we need to ask God regularly for the forgiveness of our sins, even when we are not conscious of having offended his law. But if that statement is meant to say that Christians regularly and helplessly commit sins "with a high hand," sins of willful transgression, then I must disagree on the strength of the entire New Testament, but especially Romans 6 and 1 John 1-3.

I believe it is important to keep this two-fold understanding of sin in mind at all times. Without it there is danger of falling into one ditch or another. If we make no distinction between intentional and unintentional sin, then we will be saying that Christians cannot be delivered from sinning, and we will be denying the plain statements of Scripture which I have been at pains to make clear in this book. We will suggest to one another that while God has some high ideals for our character, they cannot be realized and we must just settle for a sinning religion. The end result of that will be the situation prevailing in too much of the American church today, where leaders and people alike accept a level of behavior which is a disgrace to the Holy God. The Bible says we do not need to crucify Christ anew with our continual sinning. It says we must not. We do not need to break our Father's heart with high-handed rebellion day after day. We may live lives in which no disobedience is a part of our expectation or our practice. We may be blameless, perfect, without defect. We may be everything that could be expected of one in whom the Spirit of Jesus lives. We need not, *we must not*, sin.

On the other hand, if we forget the fact that any deviation from God's perfection is sin,[38] we may fall into the trap of believing that we cannot sin, that indeed we have arrived at that perfection which even Paul denied. We might be guilty of saying something like old-time Methodists are accused of saying, "I haven't sinned in 30 years." While such a comment may be true as regards intentional sin, it still sounds suspiciously like spiritual pride, doesn't it? Or, more dangerously, we might begin to explain away our faults and shortcomings, thereby short-circuiting all further growth. Reverting to the earlier illustration in this chapter, suppose you tell me that my ignorant comment has hurt you and I, confident that Christians do not sin, say something like this, "Well, my friend, that's your problem, isn't it? I didn't intend

---

[38]The Hebrew word translated as "sin" means to miss a target, whether intentionally or unintentionally.

to hurt you, and if you're so thin-skinned that you flare up over something like that, you need to get some help. Anyway, it's nothing to do with me." If I had not committed a sin in the sense of willful transgression before, I certainly have now! Rather, if I am conscious of the fact that any deviation from God's perfection calls for his atoning grace, I am much more likely to respond with, "Oh, I am so sorry! Please forgive me! If I had known your situation I would never have said anything like that. Please pray for me that I will become more sensitive."[39] Here is the way of growth in holiness. Here is how it is possible to be perfect in love and yet growing in love. Here is how it is possible to be perfect in obedience and yet growing in obedience.

If we keep both of these understandings of sin in creative tension in our lives, it is possible to live with a clear conscience toward God, and yet be filled with a sense of how terribly far we have to go for his complete likeness to be worked out in us. We can know that we are living in perfect obedience to his revealed will, and yet realize how little of his entire will we know. In this regard, let me revert back to two examples which we discussed earlier. The first example is that of Asa, discussed in 1 Kings 15:14. There we are told that Asa's heart was "perfect toward the LORD all his life." That is, in terms of obedience to the known will of God, Asa was all that he could be expected to be. He was completely dedicated to God. Yet, his performance left something to be desired. He did not destroy all the places outside of Jerusalem where the LORD was worshipped. We do not know why he was ignorant of this command. Perhaps if he had been a better student of the Word he would have known better. Or perhaps he should have cultivated the prophets more assiduously. But whatever the reason, this ignorance did not mar the perfection of his devotion to God. So the Bible says that he was perfect in regard to the central idea of the word "sin," that is, "transgression," whereas in the broader sense of "deviation from God's perfection," he was not.

---

[39]Such situations may often exist when persons in a majority relate to persons of a minority group.

The second example is from the New Testament. This is the one found in Philippians 3:12-15 and it is taken from Paul's life. Here, you remember, Paul says that he is not perfect and that he is perfect inside the space of four verses. In the sense of conforming to God's perfection, having arrived at all the person Paul could ever be, Paul hastens to say that he has not arrived (3:12). There is more he needs to learn about Christ, about himself, and about God's intentions for his life, and there is more of the grace of God that he needs to experience. That kind of perfection no one knows on this side of glorification. But, as we have seen, the Bible clearly talks about the possibility of being made "perfect" by God in this life. Paul agrees (he should, in view of his intent to present everyone "perfect in Christ" [Col. 1:28]), and this is why he includes himself among "those who are perfect" (3:15). How can he do this? Is he perfect, or isn't he? In the sense of being completely like Christ in his obedience and in his devotion (3:13-14), he is perfect. In the sense of needing to grow further in knowledge, wisdom, and experience, he is far from perfect.

Let me use one final illustration. Is it possible to be a perfect husband? Well, it might depend on who is asking! If one has created some absolute model of "husbandly" perfection, it doesn't seem likely that even the best of us would reach the standard. So since none of us husbands is perfect, what conclusion shall we draw? Since I am not perfect should my wife simply understand that I am going to sin against her every day? Should she simply expect that I am going to carouse with other women, "because I cannot help it"? Should she expect that I will indulge in pornography "because that's the way I am"? Should she expect me to belittle her in public "because that's just a guy thing"? Absolutely not! If it is true that there are many areas in which I need to grow as a husband, that does not mean that I therefore must break my wife's heart every day; deliberately, or even thoughtlessly, doing things I know she hates. At the same time, if I can say my heart is wholly hers without a human rival, that does not mean I can say that therefore there are no areas where I need to grow and progress. If all this is true on the human plane, how much more can it be so on the human/divine plane.

What I have been trying to say is that if we are to implement the biblical understanding of holiness in our lives, we must also have the biblical understanding of sin. Just as many cases of spiritual pride and self-deception might have been averted by keeping the two-fold nature of sin in mind, so might many cases of discouragement and despair. Many of us have tried to keep the biblical injunctions to holiness in our own strength and, having failed, as inevitably we must, have concluded that the Bible does not mean what it says. But others of us, having been taught correctly about the power of the Spirit, have indeed allowed him to fill us, but then discovered that we have fallen far short of some absolute standard which we or others had set for ourselves. Again, there was despair and the conclusion that the Bible only meant that we should *try* to be like God, knowing we never could be. But if we will keep in mind the distinction between "sin with a high hand" and "unintentional sin," much of this despair can be averted. We do not have to perform perfectly to have a heart that is wholly right with God. And because our heart is perfectly God's does not mean that we cannot be honest about our failures and shortcomings. In fact, having a heart that belongs to God completely will mean that for the first time we can really begin to get at the roots of our failures. Now that we do not need to explain away our failures or rationalize our inadequacies in order to protect our pride (the "flesh"), God is truly free to begin to work on these and to help us find his ways of overcoming them and neutralizing them.

Sin—a Matter of Disposition and Action

Not only is sin a matter of will and intent in the Bible, it is also a matter of disposition and action. This is another understanding which, if incorporated into our thinking on holiness, will make it easier for us to understand what the Bible is talking about when it calls us to holy living. We have already talked about these ideas in various ways above, but I wish to make the point explicit here.

As we noted in the previous discussion, to "sin" in the widest sense is to miss the target of God's perfect will. Thus, to lie, or to steal, or to oppress the poor are all acts of sin. They are not God's will for human behavior. Furthermore, it is not God's will that we should deify forces in the universe, and fall down to worship them. We are to give our allegiance to God alone and we are expected to live lives like his. We are not to commit acts of sin, and the Holy Spirit has come to deliver us from committing them.

But the sin that the Holy Spirit has come to deliver us from is not merely acts, it is also a disposition. In earlier chapters we talked about the fact that there is that in us which prevents us from living the life of God. This factor is called by several names. In the Old Testament it may be called the "evil imagination," or the "spirit of prostitution," although most often it is not named at all. It is simply described as that lamentable tendency in the Hebrew people to break the covenant even when they know it is a good covenant. David is referring to this tendency when he calls himself "a sinner from birth" (Psa. 51:5). In the New Testament this disposition is most frequently called "the flesh," although it is also called on occasion "the old man." As we saw in our discussion of "flesh," this term is not used to describe this disposition because the writers believed there was something sinful about the human body, or about flesh, *per se*. Rather, they used the term because this sinful attitude focuses on that which relates to the bodily desires, to physical possessions, to position, etc. Today, as we think about the "self," we might most aptly describe this tendency as self-will. But even that term probably falls short of capturing all that is involved in the Bible's thinking on the subject, because it is a self-will which is particularly intent upon denying the imposition of God's will upon it. Thus, it will choose behavior which the mind knows is self-destructive simply because to do good would be to submit to God's will.

This understanding that we have a disposition to sin explains why we cannot seem to stop performing acts of sin, and in some cases, *certain* acts of sin. And it is this disposition which prevents us from fulfilling God's expectation that we be holy people. It is not enough that our acts of sin be forgiven, because we simply commit them all over again. This situation is nowhere better described than in Romans 7. We know what is right, we want to do what is right, yet we *cannot* do what is right! Yet God expects that we be blameless in holiness before him, brides in whom there is neither spot nor wrinkle. It is no wonder that Paul cries out in frustration at the end of Romans 7, "Who shall deliver me from this body of death?"

The answer to this problem is to be found in Romans 8 and at many other places in Paul's writings especially. Not only must the acts of sin be forgiven, the disposition toward sin must be changed. If such a change is possible, then it is possible for God's people to live the holy lives they are commanded to live. Then, although they may still commit acts of sin from time to time, they will no longer be automatically inclined to do that which offends God and breaks his heart. Instead of being inclined not to do God's will, they will be inclined to do his will. Instead of being disposed to explain away that wrong behavior which stems from ignorance and character faults and to make excuses for it, they will be disposed to admit who they are in themselves and to seek forgiveness, further light (understanding) and growth.

How is it that that Paul recommends (commands!) this disposition be dealt with? In a word, death. Let us look again at Romans 8:13, "For if you live according to the flesh, you will die; but if by the Spirit you put to death the deeds of the body, you will live"(NRSV). We find similar statements in Galatians 5:16 and 24, "Live by the Spirit, I say, and do not gratify the desires of the flesh. . . . And those who belong to Christ Jesus have crucified the flesh with its passions and desires" (NRSV). The same point is made in Colossians 3:5: "Put to death, therefore, whatever in you is earthly: fornication, impurity, passion, evil desire, and greed (which is idolatry)"(NRSV). Paul is not suggesting in these statements that we simply try to stop doing certain acts of sin. He is demanding that we die to certain attitudes which produce these acts of sin. The "flesh" is that disposition in us to think that the satisfaction of our human desires for comfort, pleasure, possessions and security is absolutely all-important, and the conviction that we alone can meet those needs. This disposition is absolutely opposed to the idea that these needs are not paramount and that, in any case, the only way to genuinely meet them is to surrender them to God. The "flesh" is hideously subtle and will easily masquerade under piety as a way of hiding its total absorption with itself and its satisfaction. Thus, Paul insists that the only way to deal with it is radical. We cannot grow progressively less self-willed, he says. Rather, just as Jesus radically died to himself and his way on the Cross, so must we. As we noted above, this has already taken place in us potentially when we become Christians. But that potential must normally be brought to reality at some later point when we have finally recognized the nature of the "beast" and can now exercise faith to put into effect the death which it requires. So Paul can say that this thing *was* crucified when we accepted Christ, and at the same time, call us now to put it to death. Again let me say that "death" has an instantaneous quality about it. A person moves closer and closer to death, but there is a moment when death has unquestionably occurred. So it is with the flesh. We either are ruled by self-will or we are ruled by God's will. As Christians, those who are a part of God's kingdom, we may, indeed we must, become more and more ruled by the will of the King. But there must come a moment when we, recognizing the nature of the disposition in us, radically and forever, by God's grace, die to it. Of course there is no way we can fully understand the implications of that death at that moment, and as the ramifications of doing God's will are made clear to us in ensuing years, there will be moments of doubt and fear when that death will need to be reaffirmed. But there is only once when we fully recognize that inner opposition to the will of the One who has saved us and, in turn, absolutely renounce it, and by faith, kill it.

This is, of course, impossible for us to do in our own strength. In fact, were we to attempt to deal with this disposition in our own strength, it would only be another manifestation of the "flesh"! No, recognizing our terrible need and believing in the power of God to meet that need, we put the knife in the Spirit's hand and say, "Here, You do what I cannot. You defeat that enemy within who prompts me to do again the very things that killed you." The result will be that exultant cry of Paul in Romans 8:1-2, "Therefore, there is now no condemnation for those who are in Christ Jesus, because through Christ Jesus the law of the Spirit of life has set me free from the law of sin and death." Once we were unwilling prisoners to "the law of sin" (7:23) at work in us, knowing better, but unable to do anything about it. Now we have been set free by "the law of the Spirit of life." Now we are able to live the life of God. Now we are able to fulfill God's law, but not merely as a fulfillment of external commands. Now he has written his law on our hearts, as the prophets predicted, and our delight is to do our Father's will.

So I am saying that the problem of sin in Christians can never be dealt with thoroughly until we recognize that behind the acts of sin lies the disposition to sin, and until we allow the Holy Spirit who is in us to fulfill the potential of our conversion, crucifying that disposition in order to fill us with himself. When this happens, the ancient command of God to Abraham in Genesis 17:1, "Walk before me and be perfect," will become a reality in Abraham's children.

PART THREE

WALKING IN HOLINESS

13
Walking in Holiness

Before we close this study on the biblical foundations of Christian Holiness, I want to make some suggestions on living the holy life. These suggestions are not so much explicitly biblical as they are a drawing out of some of the implications of biblical teaching. In part, they arise from reflection upon some of the difficulties into which sincere people can get when they try to live out holiness, and we will begin with a discussion of these aberrations. When you have seen the entire list, you may have the uncomfortable feeling that you have encountered this galaxy of behaviors somewhere in the Bible. If you do have that feeling, you will be quite right. By and large, these are the behaviors of the Pharisees. Upon this revelation, remembering how harshly Jesus condemned the Pharisees, we may respond with horror, "If that's true, these behaviors must be thoroughly evil, and we should have nothing to do with anything that prompts them." But that would be an overreaction. Why did Jesus criticize the Pharisees so harshly and basically ignore the Sadducees, who had largely assimilated their faith to their own political ambitions? I suggest the answer is that the Pharisees were so much closer to the truth. Unlike the Sadducees, who were simply beyond the pale, the Pharisees were so near the truth as to be truly dangerous. They wanted to please God; they wanted to keep his covenant; they wanted to be holy people.[40] But by going about it in the wrong way, and in some cases, for the wrong motives, they brought the whole enterprise into disrepute. That was what infuriated Jesus, I think. But if we realize that these were the traps the Pharisees fell into, we will be better able to see how to avoid them for ourselves.

One of the dangers for those of us who seek to live a life that is truly holy is perfectionism. That is, because we take seriously the Bible's injunction to be perfect and without defect in our relationship with God, we begin to demand of ourselves perfect performance in every area of our lives. We listen to inspiring speakers and we read biographies of holy people, and we become convinced that they never failed or fell short of their goals (unlike us). We assume they never had difficulty discerning God's will or doing it. When they witnessed to unbelievers, we imagine, the Holy Spirit always came down in mighty conviction, and the hearers were converted. The things they liked best in all the world were to read the Bible and pray. Their homes were sanctuaries of quiet and blessing where there were never any conflicts. On the other hand, we look at our own lives and see rather different conditions. We don't always see God's will very clearly and sometimes when we do, it terrifies us and we don't want to do it. We don't always want to witness and when we do, it is not always well-received. We don't always want to read the Bible and pray. Our homes are sometimes places of tension and argument. As a result, we live with a sense of condemnation and failure.

What has happened? First of all, we have created an unreachable standard. Few preachers or biographers have intentionally set out to create a false picture of their own experience or of the experience of the one they are writing about. But they are trying to show the unquestionably good effects of the truth they are teaching and trying to persuade the hearers and readers to accept that truth for their own

---

[40]Note that while we are told that Pharisees became believers (although not without bringing problems with them!, Acts 15:5), there is no indication that the Sadducees, as a group, ever came to Christian faith.

lives. There is nothing wrong with this as a part of the art of persuasion. But because we do not see the whole picture, we think the limited picture is the whole picture. In virtually all cases, it is not the whole picture. There are failures and shortcomings, even sins. There are struggles and setbacks. To be sure, there have been those who have excelled in holy living, and it is a noble thing to seek to emulate them. But to measure our acceptance by God on the basis of absolutely perfect performance in holiness, is to condemn ourselves to failure. God is the only one whose performance is absolutely holy. The result is that we live with a constant sense of guilt and condemnation. Then, because we are afraid of failing again, we begin to stop daring for God. And in this whole process, we become increasingly fixated on ourselves and on our performance as holy people instead of on the Lord Jesus. As I will point out in more detail below, this is to slip back into a self-oriented way of living!

Coupled with perfectionism is legalism. How does one measure "perfect love"? How does one evaluate a "perfect heart"? What does "blameless in holiness" look like? Those are all rather intangible, so there is a subtle tendency to attempt to measure them by more concrete matters, such as habits, life-styles, and religious observances. How do I know I am holy? Well, because I do not use addictive substances, or because I do not dress in immodest or ostentatious ways, or because I fast and pray a lot, and am often in church.

But even these are general enough to allow a great number of variations. So there has been a tendency to narrow these down sharply in different religious groups. Thus, it is all right in some groups to smoke tobacco, but not in others. In some groups a woman could cut her hair, but not in others. In some groups a woman could wear a one-piece bathing suit, but not a two-piece. In some groups a man could not have white buttons on his clothing, but could have black ones.

To most of us today in a society where license is the norm, these kinds of things sound ludicrous. Yet there clearly are connections between outer behavior and heart condition. There were clearly instances where Paul felt it necessary to prescribe what kinds of behavior (including dress and adornment) were acceptable for

Christians and which were not. So before we too lightly guffaw at those benighted people who went before us, we need to grant that there is an important issue here. A person who says that he loves God with all his heart and yet manifestly lives for appearance, pleasure, and pride has a serious problem.

Nevertheless, holiness is first of all a matter of the heart and a matter of relationship. Whenever relationships are put on a legalistic basis, something is awry. If my friend demands that I meet him a certain number of times a day if we are to remain friends, the friendship is in trouble. If my wife demands that I account for every moment of my time when I am away on a trip, our marriage is in trouble. If my fiancee feels it necessary to buy me an expensive gift every week to prove she loves me (and to hold onto my love), she is in trouble. Holiness is a love relationship, and any attempt to quantify it will change it from the saving, freeing relationship it is intended to be into one of legalities and judgments.

That introduces the third danger: judgmentalism, which is a concomitant of the previous two problems. Because our holiness is expected to make observable changes in the way that we live, we may become perfectionistic and legalistic. We set very high standards for ourselves and those standards involve certain kinds of behavior. Of necessity, this demands measurement, and measurement means passing judgment. Thus, a large part of our lives comes to be taken up with the business of passing judgment. Again, this is not all bad. If you read the lives of many of the saints, you will see that they were very hard on themselves. They recognized that the "flesh," though crucified and no longer ruling, still constituted a temptation. As long as we live in our earthly bodies, there will be the temptation to eat too much, too pamper ourselves too much, to praise ourselves too much. To guard ourselves against these temptations and to pass judgment upon ourselves when it seems we have fallen into them is not a bad thing.

The problem arises when the whole body of our Christian life becomes absorbed with this sort of thing, which will be the case if perfectionism and legalism have come to define our experience. Then we will constantly fall short, and constantly come under our own judgment and feel that we are under God's judgment as well. When that happens, it is very common for us to engage in the psychological defense mechanisms of transference and projection. Living with a constant sense of judgment, we begin to become increasingly judgmental of others. *Our* failures are not so bad, because *theirs* are so much worse. "If only others would try as hard to be holy as I am trying." "It is terrible the things people are allowed to get away with." "Why does she get all the praise and adulation when everyone knows that I am better at what she does than she is." There are perhaps many other lines we could each add to this unhappy litany. And the really sad aspect of it all is that when we become aware that we are indulging in such ignoble behavior, then we wallow in even greater self-judgment!

All of this leads to yet a further danger. This is the danger of privatism; that is, making my holiness strictly personal and interior. It has to do with my not telling lies, my not showing anger or impatience, my not cheating, my having regular devotions, my giving a significant portion of my income to God's work, etc. These are private virtues that relate primarily to me and me alone. Again, it is clear that these are some of the fruits of the Spirit that are revealed in us when we allow him to rule in us. But the danger of these is seen in the pronoun reiterated above. That pronoun was *my*. Our enemy is not very particular about the ways in which he can get us to focus upon ourselves. He would prefer to do it by getting us enslaved to the grosser sins of the flesh. But if he can not do it that way, he is perfectly willing to do so by getting us to focus upon our piety.

This focusing upon our piety leads to another danger: introspection. We begin to ask whether we really *feel* holy or not, whether what we just did was really motivated by love or not, whether it was sinful to have had that feeling or not. We fall into a habit of self-examination and self-doubt. We wonder whether we are really making any progress in the faith or not. Again, as in the other dangers above, this is certainly not all bad. Paul challenges us to examine ourselves to see whether we are in the faith (2 Cor. 13:5). The problem comes when the self-examination begins to become morbid. The evidence of that morbidity is twofold: when we cannot stop examining ourselves and when it begins to make us lose our confidence in God's work in us. When this happens, self-centeredness has crept back in again. If, as Genesis 3 seems to teach us, self-centeredness is a result of the fall, then the experience of holiness should deliver us from that self-centeredness. How tragic if that experience in fact leads us straight back into our selves.

The last of the dangers I want to mention here is self-deception. In one way, it is the very opposite of the previous one, but in another way, it is the result of it, and indeed, of all the rest. What happens when my experience of God's holiness leads me into perfectionism, legalism, judgmentalism, privatism and introspection? I end up with a burden too heavy to carry. I have set standards for myself which are beyond what the Holy Spirit can do in me at my stage of spiritual and emotional maturity. I find myself continually falling short of what I know I should be. I withdraw into myself so that others will not see what I am really like. In the end, in order to give myself some sort of relief, I begin to deceive myself about what the real character of my life is. I begin to excuse myself and to say that what someone else might call a sin really was not, because after all, I have believed God to make me blameless in holiness, and God is faithful to do what he has promised!

Now it may be that after this dreary catalog of possibilities, the reader is thoroughly depressed. You may be saying, "If that's what seeking God's holiness will let me in for, I think I will just remain in my comfortable, sinning religion." Don't do it. Anything worth having in this fallen world has its dangers. And thankfully, that is not the level on which those who believe God's promises for their holiness must live. I have tried to alert you to the dangers precisely so that you will be able to avoid them. As the cliché has it, "Forewarned is forearmed."

So how can we avoid these dangers? How can we live the holy life in a way that is free from perfectionism and legalism, that is generous and not judgmental, that is full of justice and righteousness as well as piety, that is utterly self-forgetful and full of integrity? As I said at the beginning of this chapter, the behaviors I have been describing are the same ones that are ascribed to the Pharisees in the Gospels. Realizing that will give us some guidance on how to avoid these dangers and thus fulfill Jesus' injunction to his disciples, "Your righteousness must exceed that of the scribes and Pharisees."

If we look at the Pharisees, I believe we can see some reasons for their missing the target. First of all, their holiness was a performance. It was something that they achieved through their own rigorous self-discipline and devotion. It was something they did for God. As such, it deserved to earn approval from God. Second, their holiness was an "it." It was a concrete thing that could be weighed and measured, evaluated and judged. Therefore, it tended to be restricted to outward behaviors and to have little to do with motivations or attitudes. Third, their holiness did not presuppose faith, surrender and trust, but effort, rigor, and commitment. Therefore, it was appropriate to rate themselves and others on the level of their accomplishment. Fourth, their holiness tended to be for themselves. They were attempting to make themselves acceptable to a God who was considered to be very demanding. Thus, when they made proselytes it tended to be as a mark of their own success rather than as an expression of compassion for the lost.

With these ideas in mind, we can begin to think about ways in which to avoid the dangers for those who seek to be obedient to God's command to be holy. Above everything else, we must remember that holiness is a relationship and not an "it." When we think of holiness as a thing in itself, something to be acquired or attained, as the Pharisees did, we immediately invite trouble. Holiness is a by-product of a relationship. In a word, holiness is Jesus. Does God want us to behave in holy ways? Of course he does. It is written throughout the Bible, from cover to cover. But much more than that, he wants to live in us, and to have us live in him in a love relationship. This is what he really wants: that intimate, loving relationship that results from our complete surrender to his love and our happy obedience to his will. This is what the Pharisees were unwilling to give. They were willing to give God legalistic obedience, but they were unwilling to give him themselves. But if we will focus on Jesus, loving him, pleasing him, experiencing his life flowing through us, his holiness will be ours as a natural by-product of the relationship. So, "Am I holy?" is the wrong question. The questions are: "Is Jesus the sole, reigning Lord of my life? Is Jesus' mind being created in me? Is Jesus being glorified by my behavior? Are people being drawn to Jesus because of my life? Is Jesus becoming more beautiful, more desirable because of what he is doing in my life?" In this way we will de-emphasize ourselves, with our performance and achievements, and recognize that everything in us is as a result of his life being lived through us.

This means that holiness is a passion and not a performance. When we think of holiness as something we must do, all of the dangers of perfectionism, legalism, etc., are lurking nearby. But it is not holiness we want, it is God. In the same way, if a couple concentrates on improving their performance as marriage partners, there are danger signals flying. Let them concentrate on how to please one another, how to be more loving to each other, how to be more self-denying for the other, and there is great hope. Holiness is not something we do for God. Holiness is something that results in us because God lives there. Holiness is not a contest to see who can do it best; it is the glow on the face of one who knows herself loved without reservation. The Pharisees never learned that holiness is love in action. It is no accident whatsoever that Jesus, Paul and John all spoke of holiness as "perfect (spotless, unblemished) love." They all learned it from the Old Testament. Holiness is loving God with everything you are and loving your neighbor in the same way you love yourself. Can we love like that? Hardly! But God can give us that kind of whole-hearted devotion to himself, and that kind of self-denying, self-forgetful caring for others.

Then let us remember that holiness is a result of both crisis and process. We humans have a difficult time holding two ideas in tension. Whether it is freewill and sovereignty, or transcendence and immanence, we tend to be in one ditch or the other. It is the same here. How do we become holy? At one end of the scale is process. This was the way of the Pharisees and it has been the way of much of the Church. We struggle to "mortify the flesh," that is, to kill by starvation that rebellious self-will that is the enemy of God in us. But what is that except a refined version of the Galatian heresy? It is the flesh trying to make the flesh holy! And it will not work. It produces self-righteousness and spiritual pride, with those who have apparently attained a high level of spirituality lording it over those who have not. And behind the scenes it produces all those fruits of perfectionism, etc. which we discussed above.

Instead, John Wesley and his followers have rightly maintained that we are made holy just as we are converted: by grace through faith. But in order for that grace to become operative, there must come a moment when we surrender to God in faith for the crucifixion of our self-centered will. Typically, we are only aware for the need of such a surrender after we have sought to live for our Savior for some time. The positive side of the experience is that we surrender our entire selves to be filled with the Holy Spirit. Wesley labeled the result of this moment "entire sanctification" (1 Thess. 5:23) in order to distinguish it from the progressive sanctification which continues both before and after this moment. I am personally convinced this understanding is the one that makes the best sense of the biblical data that we have discussed in this book.

However, some of Wesley's followers emphasized this crisis experience to the virtual exclusion of process. This is very dangerous because it opens the door to a number of errors. Persons can feel that because they have had a crisis of surrender and have received the fullness of the Holy Spirit, that they have "arrived" and that no more growth is needed. Some have believed themselves incapable of sin and have denied that what was obviously sinful behavior to others was sinful in them. Some have seen the experience as an achievement of their own faith and have belittled others who did not have such faith.

So what are we to do? If sanctification by process tends to leave out the truth that God is the only sanctifier, and that holy behavior is only possible if we allow the Holy Spirit to fill us, and if sanctification by crisis tends to a kind of "us and them" mentality between those who have arrived and those who have not, what are we to do? Surely the answer is to emphasize both. On the one hand there is surely a process leading up to the crisis of surrender, death, and fullness. It is in that process of seeking to fulfill our baptismal vows that we discover our need. That is, as we have said above, a critical moment. If we do not realize that we may take a further step of faith and believe God to crucify the "flesh," we may conclude that there is nothing more for us than a life of continual struggle and defeat. But if, like Paul to the Thessalonians, someone has come either in person or through the printed word, "to supply what is lacking in your faith," then a whole new vista of life lies open before us.

Yes, in one sense Wesley is right, our holiness is "entire"; it is complete in that our surrender is complete; we are "perfect" in that there is not such a blemish on our obedience as to break our relation with the sanctifying Spirit. But what about our performance? Is this perfect? Far from it. We lack emotional and spiritual maturity. We lack wisdom. We lack experience. We may say and do things out of an absolutely innocent and loving heart which are quite wrong. This is where the process of sanctification continues. Knowing this, I do not need to excuse my terrible behavior as though I were incapable of doing anything wrong. On the other hand, I need not doubt that I am completely surrendered to God and am filled with his Spirit. What I must do is to ask the Holy Spirit to teach me through that experience so that I will not do it again. In a real way true growth in holiness is now possible in a way that it was not before the crisis occurred. Now that my will is perfectly aligned with God, he can teach me things that he never could before.

Today, as we understand more and more about the complex causes of human behavior, we know that in order for God to change some of the things we do, it may require a long process of revelation so that we understand why we are prone to do certain things. The enemy may prompt us to self-condemnation with, "You say you are a holy person? Well, I can tell you that if you were a holy person you wouldn't feel like that when people don't appreciate you. Corrie Ten Boom (or whoever) didn't feel that way." Of course that is a lie, told by the Father of Lies. But it has its effect upon us, discouraging us, making us believe that God has not really worked in our lives, and making us wonder if we should not just give up any hope of being like Christ.

There are four necessary steps here: First, we must remember again that there is nothing we can do to make God love us more than he does at this moment. Our holiness is not the cause of his love and acceptance; it is the glad response to that love. As the famous missionary to China, Hudson Taylor, learned more than a century ago, the key is rest. Rest in who Jesus is, rest in what he has done for us, rest in what he is doing in us.

The second step is to remember that the holy life is not performance, but a new set of attitudes and a new way of responding to God's love. This is what John is talking about when he says, "Perfect love drives out fear" (1 John 4:18). God has filled us with himself in the Holy Spirit. As with Paul (Phil. 3:13-14), God has made our hearts one with his, putting down the old rebellion within. That reorienting of our affections toward God is the unmistakable sign of his working, and we may put our fears behind us. When we look at the evidence of what God has done in our lives, we will "not throw away our confidence," but will "persevere so that when [we] have done the will of God, [we] will receive what he has promised" (Heb. 10:35-36).

The third step in this process of dealing with failures real or perceived, is to distinguish between sin and temptation to sin. Wesley wrote in his *Plain Account of Christian Perfection* that while he once believed that an entirely sanctified person no longer felt temptation, he had changed that opinion. While this remark is somewhat cryptic, I take it that he means that a man who has been filled with the Holy Spirit, and in whom the "flesh" has been crucified, may still feel sexually attracted to a woman who is not his wife, or that a woman who has had this experience may still feel envious of those who have received recognition she would like to have received. These are the feelings of temptation. If we did not feel them, we could not be tempted. So the issue is not whether we have such feelings, but rather, what we do with them.

There are two wrong turns which we may take at the moment when such feelings present themselves. On the one hand, we may entertain them and nurture them. This is to succumb to the temptation and to fail God and ourselves. But the other way is almost equally dangerous. We may beat ourselves for having such feelings at all, and begin to doubt God's work in our hearts. As a result we often make a vow that we will work even harder to prevent such feelings ever arising again. This is to turn toward the mentality of the "flesh," a turn which has disastrous long-term consequences. It is disastrous because it begins to lock us into a downward spiral: hating ourselves for our failures and determined to prove to God that we do not fail, we become even *more* susceptible to the whole range of temptations which fall on those who make themselves vulnerable.

If these are wrong turns, what is the right direction? Having recognized the feelings, we simply surrender them to the Holy Spirit, acknowledging that without him, we would be succumbing to all these things and more. Thus, we do not focus our attention on ourselves or beat ourselves for our supposed failures. We turn in love to our Savior, who has felt all these same things, and offer them up to him as a whole burnt offering. This is not just rhetoric. Sometimes it is hard to surrender feelings of having been mistreated or of having been ignored. So it is a sacrifice to let go of them. But this is the way of hope.

This leads us to the fourth step: self-understanding. In our new state of complete surrender to God, the process of realizing the potential for godliness, or Christlikeness, that became ours upon accepting Christ can now go on without the hindrance of an inner rebellion. What we were just describing in the previous paragraph is one of the most important phases of that growth in holiness. That phase is self-understanding. When the "flesh" was in control, we either tried to hide ourselves from ourselves, refusing to admit that we had any shortcomings at all, or we reveled in our defects, announcing to one and all, "That's just the way I am!" Now that our self is no longer on our hands, as it were, we can admit who we are without either wallowing in the shame of it or brazening it out. For the first time the Holy Spirit can begin to show us what we are really like without our fighting him. And as we come to recognize what our tendencies are and where our weak points are, the Holy Spirit is able to deal with those matters in his own creative way. Perhaps he will begin to show us from our past why some particular point is a sore one with us. He may lead us to forgive those who have hurt us in one way or another, so that we can stop blaming them and begin to accept responsibility for our behavior and attitudes. This is growth in holiness. As with physical healing, there are rare cases where God does do his deep work completely and in a moment. But just as with healing, it is much more common for this kind of sanctification to be the work of a long period of time. But I say again, this kind of an ongoing process is virtually impossible without a crisis in which we finally confront our rebellious will and make a full surrender of it, believing God to destroy the rebellion and to create in us a clean heart which is wholly his. When the crisis and process of holiness are linked in this way, we will have come a long way toward avoiding the dangers listed at the beginning of the chapter.

Finally, we will avoid many of these dangers if we remember that holiness is never for ourselves, it is for others. Why does God wish to cleanse us from our self-will and our self-centeredness? So that we can live in unbroken fellowship with him? Yes, certainly. So that we can share his character? Undoubtedly. But one of the qualities of his holy character is that it is for others. As we saw in our study of the covenant above, one of its remarkable features is that it makes fair and ethical treatment of others an act of religious devotion, an expression of our complete commitment to God. We asked why this would be so, and concluded that it is because such treatment expresses the character of the covenant Lord. This is the truth which underlies Paul's statement in Galatians that the whole law is expressed in the commandment to love our neighbors (Gal. 5:14). Whether Paul is consciously doing so or not, he is echoing the statement of Jesus that the greatest commandments are to love God and one's neighbor (Mark 12:29-31).

So why does God want to make us holy? So that, forgetting ourselves and our comfort and our prerogatives, we can handle the precious lives of those around us with clean hands. This is surely the message of Isaiah 6. Why was Isaiah given the tremendous vision of the holiness and the glory of God? Surely it was to prepare Isaiah for the ministry that was to be given him. Forcibly, Isaiah was made to see that the hope of the nation was not in human power, whether that of the now-dead Uzziah, or that of a prophet like Isaiah. The only hope was in the King, whom to see correctly was to be reduced to nothing. Yet, God does not give us a glimpse of himself in order to destroy us. Rather, his purpose is to bring us to such a level of understanding that he now can begin to deal with us seriously. So, when Isaiah saw himself and his ability as utterly nothing, it was then that God graciously cleansed that instrument which he intended to use: Isaiah's lips. Had Isaiah's communication abilities not been cleansed, Isaiah would have always been tempted to use them for himself, thinking that he was doing God and the people a great favor. The result would have been one more false prophet, afraid to speak the truth for fear of rejection and pain. It would have been like a surgeon attempting to perform surgery with a rusty, filth-covered butcher knife. The cure would have been even more dangerous than the illness!

But now, Isaiah's lips have been touched by cauterizing fire. Whatever is past is forgiven and the twistedness that puts the self above everything else has been taken away. Now whatever God puts in Isaiah's mouth to say will not be tainted by the "flesh." Isaiah will not worry about failure or success. He will not worry whether the people like him or not, or whether is accepted and approved by them. Now his love for his people is pure, it is perfect. He cares about them and not about himself. Yes, he wishes them to hear and accept the message, but no longer for his sake, but rather, for theirs. This why the chapter does not end at verse 8, where so much sermonizing on the chapter ends. Isaiah needed the cleansing fire of God precisely because he was not going to be successful in the world's terms. The message God was going to give him would not turn his own generation back to God; it would, in fact, make it more difficult for that generation to do so. But for Isaiah to preach any other message and perhaps get a superficial turning to God as happened in Josiah's time would be to mortgage the future for the sake of the present. No, for the sake of the world Isaiah had to be able to forget himself and any sentimental affection for people and declare the truth that would stand for all the ages. Only a person whose heart was perfect toward God and other persons could have done such a thing. And because Isaiah was free to do the difficult and painful thing, because he was able to forget himself, his writings, inspired by God, have stood the test of time and have shed a saving light on millions of people across 2700 years.

Like the manna in the wilderness, if we try to keep our holiness for ourselves, it will grow sour and rancid in us. But if we have learned Isaiah's lesson—that holiness is not an end in itself so that we can revel in our own purity, but is for the sake of others— then our lives will be like the widow's jug of oil which kept pouring out an unending stream of bright, pure oil. Then we will be free: free to love; free to serve; free to give; free to be self-forgetful. Then we will have begun to realize the purpose for which God made us. Then we will know that "You must be holy, because I am holy" is not a demand, but a wonderful offer.

Further Reading

Samuel Logan Brengle, *Heart Talks on Holiness*, London: Salvation Army, 1897.

Jerry Bridges, *The Pursuit of Holiness*, Colorado Springs, Colo.: NavPress, 1978.

_____, *The Practice of Godliness*, Colorado Springs, Colo.: NavPress, 1983.

_____, *The Discipline of Grace: God's Role and Ours in the Pursuit of Holiness*, Colorado Springs, Colo.: NavPress, 1994.

Charles Carter, *The Person and Work of the Holy Spirit: a Wesleyan Perspective*, Grand Rapids: Baker, 1974.

Melvin Dieter, ed., *Five Views on Sanctification*, Grand Rapids, Academie Books, 1987.

Albert Harper, ed., *Holiness Teaching Today*, Great Holiness Classics, vol. 6, Kansas City, Mo.: Beacon Hill, 1987.

Harald Lindström, *Wesley and Sanctification*, Nappane, Ind.: Francis Asbury Press, 1980 (photo-mechanical reprint with new introduction by Timothy L. Smith).

Rudolf Otto, *The Idea of the Holy*, Second edition, Oxford: Oxford University Press, 1950.

Helmer Ringgren, *The Prophetical Conception of Holiness*, Uppsala: Lundquist, 1948.

Hannah Whitall Smith, *The Christian's Secret of a Happy Life*, Boston: Willard, 1875.

Howard Taylor, *Hudson Taylor's Spiritual Secret*, ed. and Rev. Gregg Lewis, Grand Rapids: Discovery House, 1990.

John Wesley, *A Plain Account of Christian Perfection*, Kansas City, Mo.: Beacon Hill, 1966.

Mildred Bangs Wynkoop, *A Theology of Love*, Kansas City, Mo.: Beacon Hill, 1972.

Index

Aaron, 30, 36
Abel, 22, 30
Abihu, 30-31, 171
Abijah, 58
Abraham, 19, 21-26, 35-36, 48, 50, 77, 103, 106-107, 181
Achan, 171
Adam, 23, 40, 66, 169-170
Advocate, 122
Ahaz, 61, 92
Akkadian language, 17
Amalekites, 27
Amaziah, 60-61
amemphomai, 136, 143
amemptos, 158
amomos, 47
Amon, 19
Amos, 33
anaitios, 143
Ananias, 171
Anat, 18
anengkaleo, 143
anengkleytos, 144
anepilambanomai, 143
Apostle Paul, 5-6, 10, 39, 41, 81, 87, 103, 105-123, 125-126, 129-130, 132-133, 136-146, 150-164, 171, 174, 176, 179-180, 187, 189, 192, 194-195, 197
Arabic language, 17
Aramaic language, 17, 66
Archbishop Cranmer, 171
Ark, 58
Assyria, 61, 93
Atonement, 28-30, 83, 126, 137, 171-173; blood atonement, 30
Augustine, 114

Baal, 18, 42, 73
Baalam, 72-73
Babylon, 11, 71, 82
baptism, Holy Spirit, 90, 104; water, 90-91, 108
Bathsheba, 51
behavior, 2-3, 12, 14, 18, 22, 31-33, 46-51, 60-61, 69-70, 72-74, 76, 84, 93, 98-99, 105, 136-138, 143, 146, 151, 153, 155, 174, 178-179, 187-189, 192-194, 197
Bezaleel, 71
blameless, 51, 99, 136, 143-147, 150-152, 158, 162-163, 166, 174, 178, 187, 190
blood, 26, 30-31, 33, 56, 140, 143, 147, 165-168, 172-173
Boaz, 36
bondage, 24, 33, 43, 82-83, 119
"Book of the Covenant," 28-29, 45
boundaries, 13, 30, 162
Bride of Christ, 110
Buddha, 109
Burning Bush, 18, 25-26

Cain, 22, 30
Canaan, 82
Chaldees, 19
"cheap grace," 4-5
Christ Jesus, 1-6, 10, 39-40, 50, 65, 83, 86-87, 89-92, 94, 100, 103-114, 116-123, 125-133, 136-147, 152-153, 155-169, 171-174, 176, 179-180, 185-187, 191-192, 195-197
Christian Holiness Association, ix
Christlikeness, 5, 139, 158, 196
Church Fathers, 3, 114

203

condemnation, 34, 104, 106, 117, 125, 180, 186-187, 194

Confucius, 109

Corinth, 151

Corinthians, 141

cosmos, 11-15, 18, 29-31

Counselor (the Holy Spirit), 128, 131

covenant, in ancient Near East, 10, 14-17; broken covenants, 76-81; New Covenant, 79-81, 83-84, 86-87, 94-95, 121-122, 127, 140; Old Covenant, 80-81, 84, 86-87, 95, 103-104, 121, 139, 153, 178; promises in, 23-26, 34-35, 77, 93, 105, 172; purpose of, 46; sealed with an oath, 23, 26, 77; sealed with sacrifice, 23; at Sinai, 22, 24-27, 38; with Abraham, 21-26, 77; with Israelites, 19-44, 60, 62, 76-81, 107, 178, 186; with Moses, 22, 24-27, 38; with Noah, 22-23, 26

creation, viii, 13-14, 26, 30-31, 83, 121, 144

Creator, 13, 22, 38, 55, 70, 98, 161

"crisis of surrender," 193-194

Cross, 5, 33, 106, 111, 126, 128, 132, 150, 154, 163, 171, 180

crucifixion (of "flesh"), 108-109, 154, 156, 162-163, 179-180, 188, 193-195

curse of the law, 118

Daniel, 71

Dark Ages, 4

David, vii, 36, 40, 48-51, 53-54, 57-58, 67-70, 73, 75-76, 80, 83, 92, 127, 144, 178

Davidic dynasty, 55, 57, 92

Day of Atonement, 83

Day of Pentecost, 87, 128

death, 2, 10, 16, 18, 21-22, 26, 31, 35, 37, 40-41, 62, 83, 90, 103, 108, 110-112, 116-121, 126, 132, 144, 161, 164, 171, 179-181, 194

Devil, 166-167, 171

Dietrich Bonhoeffer, 4

Divine Being, 26

Egyptian, 19, 24-25, 27, 107

El, 18

Elihu, 48, 50

Eliphaz, 47

'emet, 37

Enemy, 43, 73, 76, 154, 180, 189, 193-194

Engels, 41

Enlightenment, the, 41

Ephesian Christians, 162

ethical righteousness, 27, 56

ethics, 12, 14, 16, 18, 34

Eve, 23, 40, 66, 169-170

evil, 1-2, 11, 13-14, 30, 40-41, 43, 50, 56, 65, 69, 99, 115-116, 125, 136, 158, 178-179, 185

Exile, 24, 59, 61, 78, 82, 99

Exodus, the, 17, 25-26, 28-29, 45, 86

Ezekiel, 4, 81-86, 119, 127, 162

Ezra, 99

faithfulness, 34, 37, 42, 58, 61-62, 92, 94, 99, 127, 131

faithlessness, 66, 153

"Father of Lies," 194

faultless, 46-48, 50, 144-146

fellowship, 22, 30, 33, 38, 45-46, 78, 83, 97, 104, 122, 125-126, 140, 166, 168, 170, 172-173, 197

"flesh," heart of, 81; sinful nature, 114-122, 126, 153-157, 159-161, 163-164, 177-180, 188-189, 192, 194-196

forensic holiness, 44, 109

forgiveness, 2, 5-6, 9-10, 30, 33, 81, 86, 107, 118-119, 127, 144, 154, 160, 164, 168-169, 173, 179

French Revolution, 41-42

Galatian Christians, 113, 153, 156, 163, 197

Garden of Eden, 66

Gentiles, 82, 94, 105, 151

Gibeon, 59

Gideon, 72-73

Gnostics, 159

God, character of, 2-6, 10, 13, 17, 22, 24-25, 27, 34, 36-37, 39, 44, 46, 74-75, 79, 83, 86, 97-98; holiness of, 9, 17-18, 25, 27, 33, 82, 145, 190; otherness of, 18, 20, 25, 37, 97

gods and goddesses, 11, 19, 32

Golden Calf, 28-30, 45

Goliath, 76

Gomorrah, 35

Good News, 4-5, 91, 106, 122, 151, 171

gospel, 3, 6, 90, 106, 128, 156, 164

Gospel of John, 90

Gospels, 90, 95, 128, 146, 191

grace, 1-2, 4-6, 22-24, 26-27, 33, 36-37, 40, 103-104, 106-107, 110, 112-113, 122, 129, 132, 141, 154-155, 169, 175-176, 180, 193, 201

Greeks, 114

Heaven, 50, 78, 94, 106, 121, 126, 139, 144, 157

Hebrew Bible, 35, 47

Hebrews (people), 19, 27, 34, 36, 42, 163-164

Hebrews (Book of), 23, 83, 136-137, 139-141, 143

Hebron, 53

Herrnhut, 41

hesed, 35, 37-38, 42

Hezekiah, 61-62

Hinduism, 11, 109

Hittite, 10, 15, 17

holiness, vii-ix, 1-3, 6, 9, 17-18, 22-23, 25-28, 30-35, 44, 78, 81-82, 84, 97, 132, 144-145, 156, 160-163, 165-166, 175, 177-178, 185, 187-192, 194-199, 201

Holiness Code, 28, 31

Holy Spirit, 43, 70-71, 73, 75-76, 78-80, 85, 87-92, 95, 104-105, 109, 117-122, 126, 128-132, 144, 146-147, 149-151, 155-157, 161, 163, 165, 178, 181, 186, 190, 193-197, 201; gift of, 65-85; in Old Testament, 70-82, 84-88

Hosea, 66-67

Hudson Taylor, 195

human nature, 39-44, 165

ignorance, 1-2, 22, 41, 59, 63, 170, 173, 175, 179

Incarnation, 45, 132

India, 18

integrity, viii, 34, 49-52, 190

intercessor, 122

introspection, 189-190

Isaac, 25-26, 35-36

Isaiah (Book of), 42, 69, 76, 78-79, 92, 95, 100, 197

Isaiah (prophet), 42, 56, 69, 76, 81, 85, 90-93, 95, 197-199

Israelite, 37, 82

Jacob, 25-26, 35-36, 56, 79, 103

James, 137-138

Japan Holiness Association, ix

Jehoshaphat, 61-62

Jephthah, 73

Jeremiah (prophet), 40, 79, 81, 84, 86, 121, 127

Jerusalem, 56, 59, 61, 87, 104, 143, 175

Jerusalem Bible, 107

Jeshurun, 79

Jesse, 92
Jesus Christ. *See* Christ Jesus.
John the Baptist, 90, 104, 127
Jonah, 35
Jonathan, 36
Joseph, 71, 173
Joshua, 72, 78
Josiah, 59, 62, 198
Jotham, 61
Judah, 61-62, 76, 80
Judaism, 10, 24, 39, 100, 105-107, 113, 116, 151
Judaizers, 159
Judas (Thaddeus), 130
Jude, 146
Judge, 72, 122
judgmentalism, 188-190
justice, 4, 6, 9, 56, 76-78, 92-95, 100, 190

Kadesh-Barnea, 42
katartisai, 140
King of Moab, 72
King of Tyre, 48
Kingdom of God, 120, 126, 132, 180
Kingdom of Heaven, 126
kingdom living, 127-128
kingdom of death, 112
kingdom of life, 112, 121
Kiriath-Jearim, 58

Lamb of God, 90
Last Supper, 104, 128
Last Supper Discourse, 104, 128
Law of Moses, 62
law of sin and death, 117-118, 180
legalism, 24, 187-188, 190, 192
Levites, 36, 61
Luther, 4

Maacah, 58
"The Manual of Worship," 28
Marx, 41

Mary, 73
maturity, viii, 136-139, 141-142, 190, 194
Mephibosheth, 36
Messiah, 37, 89-95, 100, 104, 128; messiahship of Jesus, 91-92; messianic kingdom, 69, 93; messianic prophecies, 92
Midianites, 42, 173
Mohammed, 109
Moses, 16, 18, 20, 22, 24-26, 29-30, 35-37, 39, 45, 62, 71-72, 77-78, 88, 98, 109, 127-128, 171-172
Mount Horeb, 22
Mount Sinai, 22, 163
Mount Zion, 87
"Mysterium Tremendum," 19, 23, 25

Nadab, 30-31, 171
nature of ancient world religions, 11-12
nature of reality, 15, 38, 44
n^ediba, 93
New Age religion, 11
New Covenant. *See* Covenant, New
new heart, 73-74, 81, 84
ne`qas, 53
Nicodemus, 65
Noah, 22-23, 26, 48, 50, 70
Nob, 59

obedience, 10, 47-48, 51, 55-56, 58, 60-63, 67, 79, 84-88, 98, 103-105, 110, 112-113, 116, 119-120, 127, 129-133, 135, 150, 167, 175-176, 191, 194
oloteleis, 145
Osiris, 19
Othniel, 73

pagan cult prostitutes (*qadishot*), 18
Passover, 29
Pentateuch, 28, 78

Pentecost, 87, 127-128, 132

"perfect heart," 49, 52-54, 57-62, 68, 75, 79, 143, 175, 187, 199

perfection, 10, 29-30, 44, 46-63, 67-68, 70, 75, 77, 79, 84, 121, 126, 135-144, 146-147, 150, 156, 163, 167, 173-177, 181, 186-187, 192, 194-195, 198-199, 201

perfectionism, 186-188, 190, 192-193

perseverance, 121, 137

Pharaoh, 71

Pharisees, 127, 185-186, 191-192

Philistines, 58

Pietists, 114

piety, 160, 180, 189-190

"Plan of Salvation," 111

pneuma, 66

polytheism, 15, 59

priesthood, 29-30, 100

privatism, 189-190

Promised Land, 21-22, 36, 42, 45, 82, 171-172

promises of God, 23-24, 105, 172

Rabbinic Hebrew, 41

rahab, 53

rebellion, 4, 37, 47, 70, 81, 115, 155, 171, 174, 195-197

Red Sea, 82

Reformation, 4

Reformers, 114

Rehoboam, 57-58

relationship with God, 10, 15, 27, 29, 32-34, 38, 57, 68, 80, 86, 103, 112, 170, 186

resurrection, 90, 108-109, 120, 132

Reuben, 173

revelation, 10, 15, 22, 27, 34, 45, 85, 90, 92, 94, 99, 105, 146, 185, 194

Righteous One, 166

righteousness, 4, 24, 27, 48-49, 54, 56, 58, 76-78, 91-95, 100, 105-106, 110-114, 116-117, 119, 122, 130-131, 136, 162, 164, 167, 169, 173, 190-191, 193

ritual, 14, 28

Romans (Book of), 5, 39, 87, 105, 113-114, 119, 125, 129, 137, 140-141, 146, 153, 156, 159-160, 164, 166, 174, 178-180

Russian Revolution, 41

Ruth, 36

Sabbath, 25, 32-33, 171

sacrifice, 22, 26, 28-30, 32, 47, 56, 76, 83, 86-87, 90, 105, 121, 127, 139-140, 145-146, 163, 166, 169, 196

Sadducees, 185-186

salvation, 4, 24, 33-34, 40, 68, 81, 103, 113, 125-127, 159

Salvation Army, ix

Samson, 73

Samuel, 59, 73

sanctification, 153, 159, 193-194, 197; process of, 194

Sapphira, 171

Sarai, 21

Savior, 43, 129, 155, 168, 193, 196

Scripture, 5, 58, 122, 166, 174

Second Coming (of Christ), 3, 153, 156-157

self-discipline, 155

Semitic language, 17, 35

Septuagint, 47, 135

servant, 47, 79, 94

sexuality, 13, 98, 154-155, 158

shalem, 52-53

shalom, 52, 78

Shiloh, 58

Shinto, 109

shophet, 72

Shuppiluluma, 17

Sinai Covenant. *See* Covenant at Sinai.

"Sinless One," 104
slm, 52
Sodom and Gomorrah, 35
Solomon, 49, 53-55, 57, 59, 68
Son of God, 100, 136, 166
Spirit of Christ, 117, 119-120, 132, 157, 160, 164; of Holiness, 78; of Jesus, 117, 129, 174, 180; of Truth, 129-132
Suffering Servant, 94
Sumer, 11
Syrians, 59

Tabernacle, 28-29, 32, 45, 58-59, 71, 137
tam, 49
Tamar, 25
tamim, 47-48, 53, 135, 137, 143
teleios, 136-143
Temple, 17, 55-57, 62, 87, 90, 112
temptation, 66, 160, 188, 195-196, 198
Ten Commandments, 34
teteleiotai, 167
Thessalonians (Christians), 143, 151, 153-156, 158-159, 194
tmm, 46, 52-53, 60
tom, 49, 53
Torah, 39, 43, 59, 62, 116
transformed life, 2, 54, 105
transgression, 47, 170, 172-175
Tribulation, 6
Trinity, 3, 91
truth, 4-5, 15, 24, 33, 35-38, 41, 48-49, 52, 62, 67, 76, 85-86, 105, 107, 121, 129-131, 137, 156-157, 166-167, 171, 185-186, 193, 197-199

Ugaritic language, 17
Ur of the Chaldees, 19
Uriah, 51
Uzzah, 171
Uzziah, 61, 198

Valley of Dry Bones, 162

Wesley, John, 149, 172, 193-195
wholeness, 34, 46-47, 49, 52-55, 58-59, 63, 66, 77, 79, 92-93, 95, 97, 112, 117, 135-138, 140-142, 145, 157-158, 164, 167-169, 175-177, 191, 194, 196-197
worship, 28, 32, 55-56, 58-59, 62, 160, 172, 178

Yahweh, 20, 35, 38, 55, 58-59, 86
Yam, 18
yasar, 49-50

Zechariah, 67, 143
Zinzendorf, 41
Zion, 56, 87, 91